Personal, Social
and
Development

Personal, Social and Emotional Development

Pat Broadhead, Jane Johnston
Caroline Tobbell and
Richard Woolley

Supporting Development in
the Early Years Foundation Stage

continuum

Continuum International Publishing Group

The Tower Building   80 Maiden Lane
11 York Road   Suite 704
London, SE1 7NX   New York, NY 10038

www.continuumbooks.com

© Pat Broadhead, Jane Johnston, Caroline Tobbell and Richard Woolley 2010

Photographs 1.1, 1.2, 2.1, 3.1, 4.1, 5.1, 5.2 used by kind permission of Paul
Hopkins - MMI educational consultancy services (http://www.mmiweb.org.uk).
Photographs 2.2, 4.3 and 6.2 used by kind permission of Emma Jordan
E-Services www.emmajordan-eservices.co.uk.
Photograph 4.2 used by kind permission of Tracy Gannon, Headteacher, Ripley
Infant School.
Photographs 2.2, 3.3, taken by Lindy Nahmad-Williams and used by kind
permission of Crowle Primary school.

British Library Cataloguing-in-Publication Data
A catalogue record for this book is available from the British Library.

ISBN: 978-1-4411-3371-7 (hardcover)
       978-1-8470-6567-4 (paperback)

Library of Congress Cataloging-in-Publication Data
Personal, social, and emotional development / Pat Broadhead ... [et al.].
    p. cm. – (Supporting development in the early years foundation stage)
  Includes bibliographical references and index.
  ISBN 978-1-4411-3371-7 (hardback)
  ISBN 978-1-84706-567-4 (pbk.)
  1. Child development. 2. Child psychology. 3. Infants–Development.
  4. Toddlers–Development. I. Broadhead, Pat, 1951- II. Title. III. Series.

HQ772.P38 2010
305.231–dc22
                                                    2010002897

Typeset by Newgen Imaging Systems Pvt Ltd, Chennai, India
Printed and bound in Great Britain by the MPG Books Group

Contents

Author Details

The authors of this book are all experienced educationalists with expertise in early years or personal, social and emotional development or both.

Richard Woolley

Dr Richard Woolley is a Senior Lecturer in Primary Education and Fellow in Learning and Teaching at Bishop Grosseteste University College Lincoln. His interests include Religious Education, Citizenship, PSHE and issues relating to inclusion, diversity and equality in primary education. Richard has taught in primary schools in North Yorkshire, Derbyshire and Nottinghamshire, including time as a deputy head and SENCO. He is a founder member of the Centre for Education for Social Justice.

Pat Broadhead

Pat Broadhead is Professor of Playful Learning at Leeds Metropolitan University. Her main area of research, conducted over the last 20 years or so, focuses on playful learning in educational settings through the growth of sociability and cooperation. Prior to working in Higher Education, she was a teacher and prior to that, a nursery nurse. Pat has a wide range of publications around playful learning and also around integrated provision for children in economically disadvantaged communities. She is just concluding 6 years as Chair of TACTYC, an early years organization for trainers and practitioners (see www.TACTYC.org.uk).

Caroline Tobbell

Caroline Tobbell has been a teacher for 24 years and has worked in a diverse range of schools in Manchester, London and Leeds. She was a Headteacher in two schools, one a primary school and one an Infant and Nursery school.

She moved into teacher Education in 2006 and currently works as a senior lecturer in Primary Education at Leeds Trinity University College where she lectures primarily on the Early Years Degree course with QTS.

Jane Johnston

Jane Johnston, one of the series editors, is a Reader in Education at Bishop Grosseteste University College Lincoln. She has worked as an early years primary classroom practitioner and in early years and primary education initial training. She has a particular interest in early years scientific development (Emergent Science) and is passionate about supporting early years development through exploration and play. Her many publications reflect this interest and she is the author of many books, articles and chapters on early years and science education, including *Early Explorations in Science* published by the Open University Press and. *Early Childhood Studies* published by Pearsons.

Series Editors' Preface

Introduction to the series

Before the 10 year strategy (DfES, 2004) and the Childcare Act of 2006, provision for children under 5 years of age was encompassed in a variety of guidance, support and legislation; *Curriculum Guidance for the Foundation Stage* (QCA, 2000), the *Birth to Three Matters* framework (Surestart, 2003), and the *National Standards for Under 8s Daycare and Childminding* (DfES, 2003). This was confusing for many professionals working with young children. The introduction of Early Years Foundation Stage (DCSF, 2008), brought together the main features of each and has provided a structure for the provision of care and education for children from birth to 5 years of age. More importantly it recognized the good practice that existed in each sector of provision and gives a framework or support for further development.

Learning in the Early Years Foundation Stage

The four themes that embody the principles of the Early Years Foundation Stage (EYFS), (DCSF, 2008) succinctly embody the important features of early years provision.

A Unique Child, identifies the importance of child centred provision, recognizing the rapid development in young children and that each child is capable of significant achievements during these years. It is important not to underestimate young children, who may be capable of action, thinking beyond our expectations. It is easy to think that children are too young or not experienced enough to engage in some ideas or activities, but we need to be open-minded as children are very good at exceeding our expectations. Some children may have particular talents, whilst others may be 'all-rounders'. Some children may have particular needs or disabilities. Each child is unique and it is our challenge to ensure that we meet their particular needs, supporting them and challenging them in their development.

Positive Relationships are essential whilst we support and challenge children so that they move from dependence to independence, familiarity to unfamiliarity, learning how to be secure and confident individuals who begin to understand themselves and others. Positive relationships are key to all areas of children's development. Emotional development requires children to have attachments and positive relationships, initially with close family members, but increasingly with secondary carers, peers and other adults. The link between emotional and social development is very strong and positive relationships will also help children to become independent and develop new relationships and begin to see their position and role in society. Positive relationships also support language development, understandings about the world, a range of skills and indeed play a part in all development.

The context in which children develop play a vital part in supporting them in all areas of development. These contexts need to be **Enabling Environments**, or environments that are secure and make children feel confident, that stimulate and motivate children and which support and extend their development and learning. The environment is made up of the physical and the atmospheric. Both need to be warm and secure, so that children feel safe and comfortable and both need to be motivating to encourage children to explore and learn. The environmental atmosphere is also created by the social interactions of all concerned, providing the security that enables a child to move away from the familiar and explore the unfamiliar in a secure and safe way. Indoor environments should provide opportunities for social interaction, language development and creative activities. Outdoor environments may encourage children to develop physically and an interest in the world around them and with opportunities to explore the familiar and unfamiliar world.

Learning and Development indicates the importance of individual children's unique development and learning. As every child is unique, so they have different learning and development needs and will develop in different ways and at different rates. It is important not to assume that all children develop at the same rate. We know that some children begin to walk or talk at a very early age, whilst others take longer, but this does not indicate what they are capable of achieving later in life. Provision for all children needs to be differentiated. In the early years, this is best done by open-ended activities and differentiated interaction and support. Open-ended activities allow children to use and develop from previous experiences and to differentiate for themselves. Support through modelling, questioning and direction can come from experienced peers and adults and will enable the individual child to develop at a rate appropriate for them.

Working within the Early Years Foundation Stage is not without it challenges. Whilst the principles recognize the individual nature of children and their needs, providing this is a different matter. The Early Years Foundation Stage encompasses children in two traditionally distinct phases of development; from birth to 3 years of age and from 3 to 5 years of age. It involves the integration of three overlapping, but traditionally distinct areas of care; social, health and education. Children will have different needs at different ages and in different areas and stages within the EYFS and the challenge is for professionals to meet these diverse needs. It maybe that the norm for children at each age and stage is quite wide and that as many children fall outside of the norm as within it. Care is needed by professionals to ensure that they do not assume that each child is 'normal'.

In order to effectively support children's development in the Early Years Foundation Stage professionals need to have an understanding of child development and share knowledge and understanding in their area of expertise with others whose expertise may lie elsewhere. Professionals from different areas of children's care and provision should work together and learn from each other. Social care, health, educational professionals can all learn from an integrated approach and provide more effective provision as a result. Even within one discipline, professionals can support each other to provide more effective support. Teachers, teaching assistants, special needs coordinators and speech therapists who work in an integrated way can provide better support for individuals. Paediatricians, paediatric nurses, physiotherapist, opticians etc., can support the health care and physical development of children in a holistic way. Early years professionals, behaviour therapists and child psychologists can support the social and emotional development of children. This notion of partnership or teamwork is an important part of integrated working, so that the different types of professionals who work with young children value and respect each other, share knowledge and understanding and always consider the reason for integration; the individual child, who should be at the heart of all we do. Good integrated working does not value one aspect of development above all others or one age of children more than another. It involves different professionals, from early career to those in leadership roles, balancing the different areas of development (health, social, emotional and educational) and ages, ensuring that the key principles of good early years practice are maintained and developed through appropriate interpretation and implementation of the Early Years Foundation Stage.

Another challenge in the Early Years Foundation Stage is to consider the child's holistic progression from birth, through the EYFS to Key Stage 1 and beyond. Working with children in the Early Years Foundation Stage is like being asked to write the next chapter of a book; in order to do this effectively, you need to read the earlier chapters of the book, get to know the main characters and the peripheral characters, understand the plot and where the story is going. However, all the time you are writing you need to be aware that you will not complete the book and that someone else will write the next chapter. If professionals know about individual children, their families, home lives, health and social needs, they will understand problems, issues, developmental needs and be better placed to support the child. If they know where are child will go next, about the differences between the provision in the EYFS and KS1 and even KS2 (remembering the international definition of early childhood is birth to 8 years of age), they can help the child to overcome the difficulties of transition. Transitions occur in all areas of life and at all ages. When we start new jobs, move house, get married, meet new people, go to university, the transition takes some adjustment and involves considerable social and emotional turmoil, even when things go smoothly. As adults we enter these transitions with some knowledge and with a degree of choice, but young children are not as knowledgeable about the transitions that they experience and have less choice in the decisions made about transitions. Babies will not understand that their mother will return soon, small children will not understand that the friends that they made at playgroup are not attending the same nursery or that the routines they have been used to at home and at playgroup have all changed now that they have gone to nursery or started in the foundation unit at school. Professionals working with children, as they move though the many transitions they experience in the first 5 years, need to smooth the pathway for children to ensure that they have smooth and not difficult transitions.

An example of holistic thematic play

Whilst sitting outside a café by the sea in the north of England, the following play was observed. It involved four children representing the whole of early years from about 2 years of age to about 8 years of age; one was about 2 years of age, another about 3 years of age, one about 5 years of age and the fourth about 7 or 8 years of age. The two older children climbed on top of a large wooden seal sculpture and started to imagine that they were riding on top of a swimming seal in the sea. They were soon joined by the 3-year-old child who sat at the foot of the sculpture. 'Don't sit there' said the eldest, 'You are in the sea, you will drown. Climb on the tail, out of the sea'. The two older children helped the 3 year old to climb onto the tail and she and the 5 year old started to slide down the tail and climb up again. Then the children began to imagine that the cars parked nearby were 'whales' and the dogs out with their owners were 'sharks' and as they slid down the tail they squealed that they should 'mind the sharks, they will eat you'. The 5 year old asked what the people sitting outside the café were and the 8 year old said 'I think they can be fishes swimming in the sea'. 'What about the chairs and tables?' asked the 3 year old, to which the older children replied that, 'they can be fishes too'.

At this point, the 2 year old came up to the children and tried to climb up the seal. The three children welcomed her, helped her climb up onto the tail and join them and asked her what her name was. They continued to play and then the mother of the eldest child came to see if the 2 year old was ok and not being squashed in the sliding down the tail. The children did not welcome the interference of an adult and asked her to go away, because 'we are playing, we are playing'. The mother helped the 2 year old to climb down off the seal and the child started to 'swim' on the floor back towards the seal and the other children. The mother said, 'Oh you are getting dirty, get up', but the child kept on 'swimming'. 'Are you being a dog' said the mother 'don't crawl', but the child shook her head and carried on 'swimming' towards the seal, avoiding the fish and sharks!

In this play episode, the children were engaged in holistic play involving aspects of

- Personal, Social and Emotional Development (cooperation);
- Language, Literacy and Communication (communicating with each other and with adults);
- Knowledge and Understanding of the World (applying ideas about animals that live in the sea);
- Creative Development (imaginative play, involving both ludic or fantasy play and epistemic play, or play involving their knowledge).

The adult intervention was, in this case, unhelpful and did not aid the play and illustrates the importance of adults standing back and watching before they interact or intervene.

Supporting development in the Early Years Foundation Stage

This book series consists of six books, one focusing on each of the key areas of the Early Years Foundation Stage and with each book having a chapter for each of the strands that make up that key area of learning. The chapter authors have between them a wealth of expertise in early years provision, as practitioners, educators, policy-makers and authors and are thus well placed to give a comprehensive overview of the sector.

The series aims to look at each of the key areas of the EYFS and support professionals in meeting challenges of implementation and effectively supporting children in their early development. The aim is to do this by helping readers, whether they are trainee, early career or lead professionals:

- to develop deeper understanding of the Early Years Foundation Stage,
- to develop pedagogical skills and professional reflectiveness,
- to develop their personal and professional practice.

Although the series uses the sub-divisions of the key areas of learning and strands within each key area, the authors strongly believe that all areas of learning and development are equally important and inter-connected and that development and learning for children in the early years and beyond is more effective when it is holistic and cross curricular. Throughout the series, links are made between one key area and another and in the introduction to each book specific cross curricular themes and issues are explored. We recognize that language development is a key element in social and emotional development, as well as development in mathematics and knowledge and understanding of the world. We also recognize that the development of attitudes such as curiosity and social skills are key to development in all areas, recognizing the part that motivation and social construction play in learning. In addition, the books use the concept of creativity in its widest sense in all key areas of development and learning and promote play as a key way in which children learn.

Although we believe it is essential that children's learning be viewed holistically, there is also a need for professionals to have a good knowledge of each area of learning and a clear understanding of the development of concepts within each area. It is hoped that each book will provide the professional with appropriate knowledge about the learning area which will then support teaching and learning. For example, if professionals have an understanding of children's developing understanding of cardinal numbers, ordinal numbers, subitizing and numerosity in problem solving, reasoning and numeracy then they will be better equipped to support children's learning with developmentally appropriate activities. Although many professionals have a good understanding of high quality early years practice, their knowledge of specific areas of learning may vary. We all have areas of the curriculum that we particularly enjoy or feel confident in and equally there are areas where we feel we need more support and guidance. This is why each book has been written by specialists in each area of learning, to provide the reader with appropriate knowledge about the subject area itself and suggestions for activities that will support and promote children's learning.

Within each chapter, there is an introduction to the key area, with consideration of the development of children in that key area from birth to 3 years of age; 3 to 5 years of age; into Key Stage 1 (5 to 7 years of age). In this way we consider the holistic development of children, the impact of that development on the key area and the transition from one stage of learning to another in a progressive and 'bottom-up' way. Chapters also contain research evidence and discussions of and reflections on the implications of that research on practice and provision. Boxed features in each chapter contain practical examples of good practice in the key area, together with discussions and reflective tasks for early career professionals and early years leaders/managers, which are designed to help professionals at different stages in their career to continue to develop their professional expertise.

Jane Johnston and Lindy Nahmad-Williams

Books in the series

Broadhead, P., Johnston, J., Tobbell, C. & Woolley, R. (2010) *Personal, Social and Emotional Development.* London: Continuum

Callander, N. & Nahmad-Williams, L. (2010) *Communication, Language and Literacy.* London: Continuum

Beckley, P., Compton, A., Johnston, J. & Marland, H. (2010) *Problem Solving, Reasoning and Numeracy.* London: Continuum

Cooper, L., Johnston, J., Rotchell, E. & Woolley, R. (2010) *Knowledge and Understanding of the World.* London: Continuum

Cooper, L. & Doherty, J., (2010) *Physical Development*. London: Continuum

 Compton, A., Johnston, J., Nahmad-Williams, L. & Taylor, K. (2010) *Creative Development*. London: Continuum

References

DCSF (2008) *The Early Years Foundation Stage; Setting the Standard for Learning, Development and Care for Children from Birth to Five; Practice Guidance*. London: DCSF

DfES (2003) *National Standards for Under 8s Daycare and Childminding*. London: DfES

DfES (2004) *Choice for Parents, the Best Start for Children: A Ten Year Strategy for Children*. London: DfES

QCA (2000) *Curriculum Guidance for the Foundation Stage*. London: DFEE

Surestart, (2003) *Birth to Three Matters*. London: DfES

Introduction to Personal, Social and Emotional Development

Personal, social and emotional development

The holistic approach recognized as the best practice by experts in early learning and advocated by the EYFS (DCSF, 2008), is underpinned in personal, social and emotional development. If children are scared, anxious, upset, lacking in confidence, have low self-esteem or feel insecure then these feelings will have a direct impact on all other areas of learning. Concentration, engagement, curiosity and interest are fuelled by security, confidence, self-worth and a mind clear of anxiety or worry. Pascal (2003) discusses the core elements of early learning which are: attitudes and dispositions; social competence and self-identity; and emotional well-being. It is clear that these core elements of early learning are centrally placed within the 6 aspects of personal, social and emotional development. The fact this area of learning and development is the first one within the EYFS (DCSF, 2008) suggests, albeit implicitly, that this is the foundation for all learning and highlights its significance. The Rose Review of the Primary Curriculum (2009) put far more emphasis on the development of personal, social and emotional skills than the National Curriculum (1999) in which there is only non-statutory guidance for primary schools. The acknowledgement of the importance of this key area of learning and the greater emphasis on emotional intelligence and emotional literacy (Goleman, 1996), which is related to the way we understand our own emotions and response to others' emotions, was a positive move forward in embracing a more holistic approach to learning.

If we consider the outcomes in Every Child Matters (DfES, 2004), the need for children to be safe and healthy (including mental and emotional health), enjoy and achieve and make a positive contribution, these cannot be achieved without personal, social and emotional development. This area of learning will be affected by the daily interactions within our settings, the ethos, the values and the way in which we support transitions to provide a secure and nurturing environment. A headteacher of a primary school for children with emotional and behavioural difficulties calls the children in her school nurture children. This is to emphasize the need for her setting to provide the aspects of nurture that many of the children have missed in their early years which may well have contributed to their difficulties in handling their emotions and becoming socially unacceptable within mainstream schools. The aim of this book is to support professionals in developing the 6 aspects of personal, social and emotional development to provide children with strong foundations on which to support and promote all other aspects of learning.

Holistic development in personal, social and emotional development

Three five-year-olds were building a church with the wooden bricks. They had built the base and were building it up to make a church spire.

> J: We need more blocks.
> M: I've got some.
> L: No, they're too big. It will topple over! These, these (getting smaller bricks out of the box).
> J: They are the same.
> L: No – look – thy are smaller (lining up the smaller block against the bigger block).
> J: Oh yeh ! Use those.

M: I want some (trying to snatch some from J) Give me them!
J: No. Get some out of the box. There are more in the box.
L: Look here are some more. (M takes them.)

The children continue building with the blocks sometimes looking anxious if it appears to wobble.

J: We need a pointy one.
L: Here's a triangle.
M: Yeh – that's good. Put it on.

L balances the triangular block on the top and the children look at their church with satisfaction. They continue to play with their church for a further 15 minutes. They talk about a drawbridge but one child says that it would be a castle with a draw bridge. They make a door that opens and shuts and 2 children have a long discussion about ensuring the dog can get out of the church through the door. The other child says there isn't a dog but is told it is a pretend dog. One child talks about gravestones and puts some blocks to represent graves. Another child goes and gets some dolls from the dolls house and pretends they are getting married.

This child-initiated play demonstrates a number of aspects of personal, emotional and social development. All three children have the confidence to voice their feelings and ideas. They play well together showing that they have formed positive relationships and friendships and when there is a conflict, this is quickly resolved by the children. There is cooperation and independence, both during the building of the church and in the subsequent imaginative play. They respect each others' ideas and help one another in a shared venture. Other areas of development can also be identified:

- Communication, Language and Literacy (see Callendar and Nahmad-Williams, 2010) – The children use language for communication and language for thinking by speculating, instructing, explaining, expressing a need, justifying.
- Problem-solving, reasoning and numeracy (see Beckley et al., 2010) – The children show a clear understanding of shape and size and a professional observing might note that they could give the children access to more mathematical vocabulary in future sessions.
- Knowledge and Understanding of the World (see Cooper et al., 2010) – There are a number of aspects demonstrated including an understanding of design, construction and balance, knowledge about buildings and their uses, knowledge of religious ceremonies.

- Physical Development (see Cooper and Doherty, 2010) – The children are very careful when balancing the bricks, understanding the need for careful and controlled movements, both when using their hands and to be spatially aware when near the church. This is extended when making the door that can be slid open and closed.
- Creative Development (see Compton et al., 2010) – The children are involved in imaginative play, sometimes fully immersing themselves in the play and sometimes showing a recognition of the pretence, such as when talking about the dog.

Structure of this book

In Chapter 1, Dispositions and Attitudes, Richard Woolley discusses issues such as respect, fairness and caring to support the development of self-worth and personal identity. In Chapter 2, Self-Confidence and Self-Esteem, Richard Woolley explores how children learn to relate to others in cooperative and collaborative ways, highlighting how the establishment of good relationships is a fundamental part of developing the confidence to learn and grow. There is also a consideration of how children learn to handle success and elation and frustration and failure. In Chapter 3, Making Relationships, Pat Broadhead discusses her research into children's play and how friendships are built through play, with consideration of resources, objects, artefacts, language, problem-solving and conflict resolution. In Chapter 4, Behaviour and Self-Control, Caroline Tobbell discusses the importance of adults understanding how children's development affects their ability to control their behaviour. There is a consideration of professionals' understanding, responses and skills in managing behaviour. In Chapter 5, Self-Care, Jane Johnston looks at the development of self-care, children's growing independence and how this can be supported by adults. Issues such as making choices and solving problems are explored to show how children can be encouraged to take increasing responsibility for their own needs. In Chapter 6, Sense of Community, Richard Woolley concludes the book with a consideration of the ways we can support children in appreciating difference and diversity, developing a sense of community and the importance of respecting others.

The case studies and reflective tasks will also help professionals to reflect on their own practice, consider the theories and research underpinning effective practice and enable them to identify how they can (and why they should) develop their practice. These case studies are designed at two levels; the early career professional and the early years leader. The early years professional may be a student/ trainee who is developing their expertise in working with young children and, for them, the reflective tasks encourage them to look at the case studies and engage in some critical thinking on issues that are pertinent for early years education. They will also be able to use the chapters to develop their understanding of issues in knowledge and understanding of the world and try out some of the ideas to develop their skills supporting children in this important area of development. The reflective tasks for early career professionals are also relevant to professionals who are in the early part of their career and to help them in their day-to-day interactions with children but also to help them to engage in the national debates about good practice and educational theories. The second level of reflective tasks are geared towards the early years leader, who has a strategic role to develop the practice of those who work with them but also the children in the early years setting. They would be interested on the impact on both the adult professional development but raising standards in knowledge and understanding of the world in young children in their setting. The reflective tasks may well be ones that can be addressed as part of a staff meeting or staff development session and can follow the practical tasks so that professionals at all levels can share ideas and experiences, identify factors affecting their support for children, both positive factors and challenges to overcome. In this way professionals can discuss their own and other's practice, share successes, support each other and come to realize that there is not one model of good practice, one recipe, that if we all follow will automatically lead to success in children's development and help the setting achieve outstanding recognition in inspections.

We hope that professionals reading this book both enjoy and find the content useful in their professional lives.

References

Beckley, P., Compton, A., Johnston, J. and Marland, H. (2010) *Problem Solving, Reasoning and Numeracy*. London: Continuum

Callander, N. and Nahmad-Williams, L. (2010) *Communication, Language and Literacy*. London: Continuum

Compton, A., Johnston, J., Nahmad-Williams, L. and Taylor, K. (2010) *Creative Development*. London: Continuum

Cooper, L. and Doherty, J. (2010) *Physical Development*. London: Continuum

Cooper, L., Johnston, J., Rotchell, E. and Woolley, R. (2010) *Knowledge and Understanding of the World*. London: Continuum

DCSF (2008) *The Early Years Foundation Stage; Setting the Standard for Learning, Development and Care for Children from Birth to Five; Practice Guidance.* London: DCSF

DfEE (1999) *The National Curriculum: Handbook for Teachers in England.* London: DfEE/QCA

DfES (2004) *Every Child Matters: Change for Children in Schools.* London: Department for Education and Skills

Goleman, D. (1996) *Emotional Intelligence.* New York: Bantham

Pascal, C. (2003) 'Effective early learning', in *European Early Childhood Education Research Journal,* 11(2) 7–28

Rose, J. (2009) *The Independent Review of the Primary Curriculum Final Report.* Nottingham: DCSF

Dispositions and Attitudes

1

Introduction

Practitioners need to nurture a child's sense of self and to help them to understand that they are unique and special. This can help with the development of an understanding that all people are special and need to be treated with respect, care and fairness. This process involves the socialization of young children, enabling them to understand the norms and expectations of the world around them. Learning what behaviours are appropriate in given situations, how to act in polite ways and how to keep themselves safe, are all important aspects of this learning process; questioning these norms is also an important part of learning. The learning process involves listening to others, turn taking, allowing others to share resources and playing cooperative games. Children need to be encouraged to try new things in order to grow in experience and gain additional knowledge, skills and understanding.

It is essential to create safe and secure learning environments, in which children feel able to take appropriate risks in a supported and supportive setting, so that children are motivated to learn without the fear of failure. Children also need to know that their ideas are valued and valuable and to understand that they deserve to receive, as well as show, respect to others. Understanding what is right and wrong is a central part of this process, drawing on the notions of respect, fairness, care and being safe. This chapter uses examples to consider how children can gain an appropriate sense of trust, how ownership and sharing affect the use of resources, and how it is sometimes necessary to say sorry or accept an apology from others. The chapter considers issues relating to theories of child development and how children move from focusing on their own needs towards considering those of others.

Exploring terms and child development

The word disposition is strange. We sometimes talk about people who are disposed to being optimistic, content or happy. The term suggests an inbuilt tendency or reaction to circumstances; it can infer that we have a natural propensity to certain responses or attitudes. It is not the purpose of this chapter to explore the whole nature versus nurture argument; this debate has been ongoing for decades and continues to fascinate students of child development and psychology. In this chapter the word disposition relates to the temperament of a child: the ways in which they react, relate and respond to internal and external stimuli. It is sometimes used in the context of talking about a person's natural tendency to behave in a particular way. I have encountered young children who are resilient and others who lose confidence quickly: their temperament seems disposed to certain reactions in the circumstances they encounter. As professionals we need to consider where such dispositions come from and how we can help children to develop positive dispositions and attitudes. The word attitude is less problematic, focusing on the ways in which we approach or regard a situation. At times it is used in a rather sweeping manner that brands the whole of an individual's personality: 'He has a bad attitude!' This is not the intention of this chapter and is why it relates to attitudes rather than a singular attitude.

Dispositions, like other personal and social behaviours, are learned through early experience, and can be un-learned through subsequent experience

(Brooker and Broadbent, 2003). While studies have shown that heredity does seem to influence temperament (e.g. Kagan, 1992; Freedman and Freedman, 1969) the degree of its influence depends on the parents' responsiveness to their children and other environmental factors in childhood (Santrock, 2007). Children who are naturally shy are more likely to display this temperament in the early years setting if their parent/carer has been critical of the trait than if they have been accepting of it (Rubin, Burgess and Hastings, 2002). Theorists debate the relationship between temperament and personality (Bee and Boyd, 2003) and it may be that temperament is effectively the emotional foundation of personality (Rothbart and Bates, 1998; Berger, 2000). Personality may be shaped by the ways in which a child's temperament is regarded and responded to by those around them.

Researchers who study adult personality have identified five basic dimensions of temperament that underline personality in humans (Digman, 1990; McDonald, 1995; McCrae et al., 1999):

- extroversion: the tendency to be active, assertive and outgoing;
- agreeableness: the tendency to be helpful and kind;
- conscientiousness: the tendency to conform and be organized;
- neuroticism: the tendency to be anxious, moody and self-punishing;
- openness: the tendency to be imaginative, curious and to welcome new experiences.

These traits are also identified in studies of children in different locations around the world, and may provide an indication of the temperaments innate to all people (Berger, 2000). However, how someone develops this nature into personality is affected by the context into which they are born and their early experiences. While these five labels for temperament may help us to consider a child's dispositions it is not helpful to attach a specific label to a child. Rather, the descriptions drawn from studies may provide us with ideas to consider the dispositions of a child, which will help as we try to meet their specific needs on an individual basis.

Dispositions and attitudes from birth to 3 years of age

In their first year, children begin to develop an understanding and awareness of themselves. They learn that they can influence others including by communicating when they need feeding, changing or sleep. They enjoy the opportunity to receive an adult's undivided attention for times of play. They also understand that they can be influenced by others by being comforted, cuddled, rocked, fed and reassured. They develop self-awareness by exploring their own movements and their immediate environment (Papalia, Gross and Feldman, 2003). How others react to children during this phase of development can have a significant impact on the development of their attitudes and the ways in which they respond to both people and their environment.

From 8–20 months children gain a greater sense of self as being separate from others. Indeed, from the ages of 4 or 5 months they will have started to focus on objects that do not involve their mother (Hughes, 2002). By 18 months they will have developed a sense of object permanence (knowing that when things are out of sight they still exist) and person permanence (an internal appreciation that people continue to exist as time passes and as they are in different settings or situations) (Smith, Cowie and Blades, 2003). During this phase their sense of personal likes and dislikes develops and their ability to explore, roll and move increases. At this stage they will play with toys placed near to them and with their own fingers and toes. The can enjoy seeing themselves in a mirror and are able to make choices: research by Lewis and Brooks-Gunn (1979) suggests that from the age of 18 months children appreciate that the image in the mirror is their own; and providing opportunities to select from different healthy snack choices provides one way of encouraging decision-making and exploring preferences. Feeling safe and supported when making choices and exploring their immediate surroundings provides the opportunity to gain a sense that discovery is positive and can feel very satisfying. This is an important part of nurturing the child's innate dispositions (or temperament) and developing positive attitudes.

Attachment

One positive attitude that develops early in life is the child's attachment to a significant adult or caregiver. Understanding this bond provides an indication of their social and emotional development; secure attachment plays an important role in the maturation process and helps children to form appropriate relationships later in life (Bowlby, 1951). Between the ages of 1 and 2 years it is possible to assess infant attachment by observing children in a 'strange situation' (Ainsworth et al., 1978; Main and Solomon, 1990). The strange situation has been used often in research, and involves observing the mother playing with the child, leaving the child alone by exiting the room and seeing how the child responds to a stranger entering the room. Commonly, four kinds of attachment are identified:

- secure attachment,
- avoidant attachment,
- resistant attachment, and
- disorganized/disorientated attachment.

Those experiencing secure attachment will be comfortable exploring new surroundings, using their mother or primary carer as a safe reference point to which they can return. They will cry if their mother leaves and not be easily comforted by a stranger; when the mother returns securely attached infants will seek them out and be easily comforted. Children that prefer closeness to the carer, rather than exploring their surroundings, are described as having resistant attachment. They will become extremely upset when their mother leaves the room and will show continuing distress when she returns. Some children will appear indifferent and play independently in a new situation without responding to their mother's comings and goings; they will be no more responsive to their mother than to a stranger in that situation. This is termed avoidant attachment. Disorganized/disorientated attachment is shown when infants react to the strange situation in ways which seem confused or contradictory. They may stare blankly at their mother or not approach her on her return, or they may cry for periods for no particular reason. This is believed to be the most severely insecure form of attachment.

It is important to note that the strange situation test only shows the sense of attachment in that particular situation and that children may respond differently in other contexts or settings. It only shows a snap-shot of their dispositions and attitudes, albeit an important one. In addition, the level of attachment shown may be affected by cultural differences. For example, in some cultures children are encouraged to be independent from an early age (e.g. in Germany) and may thus mistakenly appear to exhibit avoidant attachment (Grossman et al., 1985). In other cultures it would be extremely rare for the mother to leave the child at any time (e.g. in Japan) and so the strange situation may give the child a sense of utter abandonment (Miyake et al., 1985; Takahashi, 1990).

By 24 months children who have developed a secure attachment will have also developed many positive cognitive and emotional traits (Hughes, 2002). The reassuring feedback given by their caregivers will have developed their sense of self-confidence, self-worth and personal ability. This lays an important foundation to support the development of healthy and positive relationships in the years that follow, including the ability to seek and receive care and to give care to others.

From 16–26 months children develop their curiosity further and enjoy learning new skills. It is important to reinforce particular qualities and skills in order to build the sense that the child is unique and special (DCSF, 2008a, 2008b). Parents, carers and professionals can do this by telling the child what they are good at and by affirming positive traits: 'You are happy today', 'What a lovely smile', 'I love it when you help me', 'What a good choice'. From 22 months particular preferences, characteristics and interests develop more strongly. Professionals are able to observe the choices that children make and what they chose to do or not to do, as illustrated by the case of Anna below. Children's preferences can last for varying amounts of time and provide information to help professionals and other adults to plan further experiences for the child. By the age of 2 years children will have some sense of personal performance standards for their behaviour and will experience personal pride or shame depending on how well they meet these standards (Hughes, 2002). Encouraging engagement and providing opportunities for quality social learning are important as children can develop a good deal of self-assurance during this phase.

Case study

Anna is aged 26 months. The early years professionals in her nursery have noticed that she does not engage with making choices. If a variety of biscuits are on the plate at break time she will not take one, but she happily eats a biscuit if it is given to her. Similarly, if several toys are laid out on the carpet she will not take one, but rather sits and watches the toys and others playing with them. If the element of choice is taken away, or if she is given a specific toy, she plays happily and shows a good level of imagination in her play.

Reflection for early career professional

- How might you encourage Anna to make choices?
- What interventions or strategies might support the development of self-confidence and a positive attitude?
- What factors might be affecting Anna's ability to choose?

Reflection for leader/manager

- How do you encourage professionals to provide a range of choices so that children can develop independence and positive dispositions?
- Evaluate your approach to transition, considering how children are supported when being introduced to the highly stimulating environment of your setting.
- Observe and evaluate how your colleagues present children with choices and whether this provides children with genuine options or restricted opportunities.

Dispositions and attitudes from 3 to 5 years of age

As they reach the age of 3 years children enjoy new experiences and have a positive approach to activities. They are becoming increasingly independent in selecting and engaging in activities and show confidence in working alongside others (DeHart, Sroufe and Cooper, 2004). Adults are able to support children's interests and to become their partners in learning. Children are able to manage resources with increasing independence and should be allowed to use and care for materials on their own when possible. Making materials accessible to children supports choice-making and independence. Such child autonomy is very much in the tradition of the High/Scope curriculum (Hohmann and Weikart, 2002).

From 40 months until the age of 5 years children can persist in activities for increasing levels of time and show high levels of involvement. They are able to complete activities to their own levels of satisfaction and appreciate being able to pursue tasks without interruption. They are able to face increasingly challenging activities and benefit from a structure that helps them to achieve progress in small steps. Concentration increases and children are able to listen to others for longer periods of time (DCSF, 2008a). Supporting activities that allow both speaking and listening helps to develop concentration and engagement. Around this time a child begins to realize that we cannot see what she has seen or know the things that happened when we were not with her. This can lead to telling lies and it is important to talk with children about truthfulness and the need to be honest about events – even when we have not seen them. A child may presume that we have seen all that they have, talking as though you shared their experience. She may tell you about the park as though you had been there with her or remember the dog she saw on the way home even though it was Grandma, not you, who collected her from school (Einon, 2001).

Self-Awareness

From around the age of 4 children begin to understand the existence of mental states in themselves and others. They have an increasing awareness that feelings, intentions, desires and beliefs can exist in the mind. Theorists refer to this as a 'theory of mind' (Astington, 1993; Premack and Woodruff, 1978). An understanding of others' feelings and perceptions and being able to recognize emotions in others is a fundamental part of interpersonal relationships (Puckett and Black, 2001). As children develop a theory of mind they begin to enjoy more socially satisfying interactions with others. Appreciating the thoughts of others can be supported through role play and other imaginative play, through the use of stories which detail the feelings of various characters, and through give-and-take in relationships with friends and siblings. This can help to nurture feelings of care and empathy.

By 5 years of age children still have some major fears but these are coming to be of more concrete situations than of ghosts under their bed (DCSF, 2008a). Fears may include being separated from you, thunder and lightening, the dark, snakes and insects. Many or most of these fears will pass over time. Children in this phase are becoming more independent and love to have a sense of responsibility, for example choosing their own clothes or giving money to a shopkeeper. They are developing a sense of their own style, and are often disposed to spotting the most expensive item on the toy shelf, and to identifying what they think they can do by using the statement, 'I can ...' This may include anything from doing the washing or ironing to making a meal; often a huge amount more than they are ready to do just yet. This sense of being more grown up is also reflected in the ability to concentrate or look at books and play independently for increasing amounts of time, sometimes up to 20 minutes. This is a period of enjoying life and seeing the best in people and children are often described as having a 'sunny disposition'.

Case study

I observed John during a painting activity in a Reception class. He was working independently at an easel producing a picture of his house as a part of thematic work on *Our Homes*. He used a variety of small and large brushes to produce varying detail and chose a good selection of bright colours from the available range of ready-mixed paints. He was able to represent a traditional house with a central door, a window in each of the four corners, a roof, chimney and a block of colour below to represent a lawn. John showed that his fine motor skills were developing very well and that he had a strong awareness of some of the main elements of the building.

When the picture was completed John took it off the easel. I thought that he was going to place it on the drying rack but instead he screwed it up and put it in the bin. He started to paint again and produced a very similar representation of a house. As he began to take this finished picture off the easel I felt that his persistence and achievement required acknowledgement and went over to John to give praise. 'It's rubbish,' he said, 'my house is nothing like this one.' Before I could react he screwed up the painting and put it in the bin.

Reflection for early career professional

- What does this case study suggest about John's attitudes and self-confidence?
- What interactions could you develop to give reassurance or affirmation to John?
- What strategies might help John to refine his painting so that he finds it more acceptable?

Reflection for leader/manager

- How do you encourage practitioners to observe and monitor children's dispositions and attitudes during independent activities?
- John has a good degree of self-awareness but his skills do not match his expectations of himself. What strategies would you suggest to colleagues so that they can give John honest and constructive support?
- How would you support a colleague who came to you with concerns about John's development? What resources or partnerships might provide effective support?

Transition to Key Stage 1 (5 to 7 years of age)

The transition from the Early Years Foundation Stage (EYFS) to Key Stage 1 brings increased opportunities to learn about more unfamiliar situations and ideas that are more distanced from the child's immediate experience. In order to build on the curriculum for the EYFS it is essential to maintain a focus on the development of skills rather than refocus on a knowledge-based curriculum. It is important to maintain and nurture a child's positive disposition towards learning and to support the child in the further development of a sense of right and wrong, ways of maintaining positive interactions and friendships with other children and independence in the care for and use of resources. Increasing levels of choice bring further independence, although professionals need to ensure that skills are scaffolded so that children can become familiar with the different pedagogical approaches and structure of teaching in Key Stage 1.

With greater independence comes increased responsibility for one's own actions. One way of developing responsibility for learning is through self-assessment. While discussions with children about the activities they have completed can be time-consuming, particularly initially, they are an important part of helping children not to rely solely on the teacher's view of their work or on the need to please the teacher rather than to explore their own creativity and abilities. Developing a child's responsibility for their own behaviour and helping them to understand that their actions affect others are important parts of helping them to become increasingly independent. This helps them to understand that respect for others and for property is to be shown even when an adult is not supervising them.

Case study

Children in a Year 2 class have been complaining that small items have been going missing. Today alone an eraser, three pencils, a hair band and small toy have disappeared. Children are becoming upset when these personal belongings cannot be found. During the afternoon break you decide to look in the children's individual trays to see if the items can be found. You discover all the items, and several others including items from your own desk, in Zara's tray.

Reflection for early career professional

- How would you approach this situation with Zara?
- What action would you take and what other people might you involve or consult?
- How would you respond to Zara's repeated denial that she took the objects and to her suggestion that another child placed them in her tray?
- Would your knowledge of Zara's temperament and attitudes help you to judge the situation and influence how you spoke with her?

Reflection for leader/manager

- How would you advise a colleague who comes to you with concerns that items are going missing in their classroom?
- What immediate concerns does Zara's situation raise? What concerns would you have about advising a professional to speak with her parent/carer?
- What policies to you have in place to deal with low self-esteem, attention-seeking behaviours or disputes arising between children? How do you communicate these to fellow professionals and monitor their effectiveness?

Respect, fairness, caring and staying safe

Respect is an attribute that affects a number of dimensions of our lives. First there is respect for ourselves: understanding that we are special, unique and precious and that we deserve to be looked after and need to look after ourselves. Second, there is respect for others, appreciating that we should treat them as we would wish to be treated ourselves. Third, there is respect for our environment: taking care of resources; understanding that some items belong to other people and may not be for our use or consumption; and ensuring that those in our group get an equitable share by being listened to and allowed to speak, taking a turn on play equipment or each receiving fruit during snack time. Fairness is a useful concept to use when helping children to develop respect, by asking a child whether they felt their actions or words were fair to another child. Using questions can help children to think through the consequence of their words and actions and to begin to internalize an understanding of how to behave towards others in a range of situations.

Children who grow up in loving, caring environments find it easier to learn to care than those brought up in unemotional, aggressive or manipulative settings. The ways in which they treat other people is modelled on the behaviours of those around them. A loving carer or professional may go some way towards compensating for negative parenting (Einon, 2001). Most preschool children are kind, helpful, affectionate and thoughtful but rivalry and lack of consideration can increase once they enter the more competitive world of the learning setting.

Sometimes we will need to address issues of care or fairness with children. Our responses (actions and words) can help by modelling the care and respect we would like the child to show. I recorded the questions used by Lynn as she tried to resolve a situation in a nursery class:

- Was it fair to take five of the dolls for your game?
- Did you really need so many toys?
- Would it have been kind to leave some of the toys for other children?
- How do you think Jane felt when she didn't have a dolly to play with?
- What do you need to do to make Jane feel better?
- Would you like to choose one of the dolls to play with now?

Photograph 1.1 A baby interacting (© P. Hopkins)

This series of questions provided the opportunity for the child to think about their own actions, to reflect on whether they had been greedy with the resources, to consider the needs of others, to find a resolution to the situation, to offer an apology and to make amends, and to end the process in a positive way by making an appropriate choice and moving on from the situation. The initial questions infer a correct answer is expected, but the later ones are more open and provide the chance for the child to think through their actions and the associated consequences.

Empathy and cooperation

Children in the Reception class will be developing the ability to show care and empathy and can be supported in making amends by saying sorry. When another person is clearly distressed or upset or feeling unwell they are able to show concern and consideration, although they may not be able to spot less obvious indicators of discomfort. In one class I saw how children cared for David during an afternoon visit to the setting after breaking his leg. They were keen to bring him toys to play with, to give him hugs and a couple of the children made cards for him to take home. They were aware that he would not be able to attend regularly for some time and wanted to show their care and concern to him. While this might be appropriate for a short visit it might become overpowering if experienced for a prolonged period of time and children may not be able either to maintain the level of care and attention or to

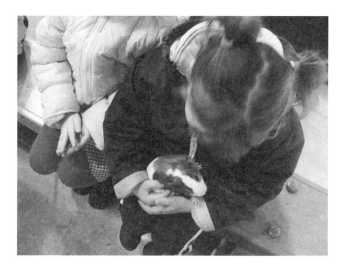

Photograph 1.2 Caring for pets (© P. Hopkins)

understand how to develop their actions over time so that they become more appropriate and gently supportive. Behaviours such as empathy and altruism (helping others without the expectation of reward) are termed prosocial behaviours (Puckett and Black, 2001; Bee and Boyd, 2003). Prosocial behaviours are particularly encouraged where children see such behaviour modelled by others and where they have experienced nurturing themselves. In general their frequency increases throughout the preschool years (Eisenberg and Fabes, 1998), although some behaviours, for example comforting another child, appear to be more common in preschool and the early years foundation stage (Eisenberg, 1988).

By the age of 5 years children enjoy playing games and cooperating with others, although this can be complicated by their desire to make up their own rules. While there is a developing sense of fairness this can focus more on the wish for others to conform to their own expectations and requirements than a mutually reciprocal balance of needs. They love to tell jokes and stories and to repeat these, although they may not yet have grasped the need to include a plot or a punch line. They will have a vocabulary of around two thousand words and be able to construct sentences of around ten syllables. They will enjoy using their language skills and often find words and ideas highly amusing and expect adults to join in the humour, even when it is effectively lacking from their conversation. These abilities all show a positive attitude to learning and an enjoyment of trying our language and seeking to develop relationships and to engage with others.

The Early Learning Goals (DCSF, 2008a:12) that I identify as relating particularly to children's dispositions and attitudes at the end of this phase are to:

- continue to be interested and motivated to learn;
- maintain attention, concentrate and sit quietly when appropriate;
- understand what is right, what is wrong and why;
- consider the consequences of their words and actions for themselves and others;
- understand that they can expect others to treat their needs, views and cultures and beliefs with respect.

Importantly, these benchmarks include an understanding that respect should be reciprocal which helps to support a developing sense of self-worth and personal identity. Jane Johnston develops these themes further in Chapter 5 on Self-Care.

Respect and fairness can be nurtured by developing an understanding of the importance of honesty. Adults can do this by modelling the process through their own behaviour, reasoning and explanation. Reading or making up stories which illustrate people's experience of being honest and making mistakes can support this process, as can thinking aloud, describing your feelings when you make a mistake and admitting shortcomings. This can provide children with phrases and responses that will support them when they face difficult situations and will help them to develop coping strategies so that they do not over-react to failure or accidents.

Practical tasks

Develop a role-play situation in which you present a character that is worried because they have broken a special item belonging to a parent, carer or friend. Ask the children to offer advice and to suggest different ways of dealing with the situation.

- What do the children's responses suggest about their developing sense of right and wrong?
- How did the children respond to one another's ideas?
- Did the children draw on experience from other settings, from their own experience or that in stories?
- Could the children suggest possible consequences resulting from the resolution strategies they suggested?

Developing a sense of self-worth and personal identity

Jason and Sarah, aged 4, devised the following poems by suggesting ideas to complete the two words starting each line:

> I am . . . Jason and I am four
> I can . . . count up to ten
> I think . . . about my cat a lot
> I want . . . to ride a bike on my own
> I like . . . to eat pizza with my sister
> I am . . . Sarah

I can . . . write my name like this
I think . . . that clouds are like cotton wool
I want . . . to be a doctor
I like . . . to stroke my cat and give it treats

This process provided positive statements for Jason and Sarah to consider their own identity, likes and abilities and to speak about themselves and decide what ideas were important to write down. Sarah found it hardest to decide what her special thought would be and Jason took a while to consider what his want was. It is interesting that both included their name in the 'I am . . .' statement and this reinforces the importance of names as being a special part of our identities. The poems show how children of this age can share concrete descriptions of observations of self. They are not yet able to process abstract concepts and to identify themselves in terms of actual personality traits (Hughes, 2002). While children from the age of 3 years 6 months will describe themselves in terms of typical emotions and attitudes, 'I'm happy when I ride my bike,' and 'I don't like visiting the farm,' they do not refer directly to personal traits, for example 'I am shy' (Heyman and Gelman, 1999; Berk, 2006).

Developing a sense of personal identity is an ongoing process from birth. As is outlined above, finding out what we can do, what we like and dislike is an important part of the learning process. Knowing such preferences is a key part of finding out who we are and what it means to be Jason, Sarah or Richard. While this may be a life-long process, the learning that takes place in the early years lays the foundations for how we will see ourselves during later growth. Making positive statements to children and affirming their efforts, achievements and attributes is a key part of nurturing and reinforcing this development of self. As the sense of self develops, so it becomes possible to develop a sense of self-esteem, which represents a degree of self-judgement. At around the age of 4 years children typically have unrealistically high self-esteem and overrate their ability to do many tasks, even in the face of failure. This can be a great motivational asset at this stage. By 5 or 6 years they are comparing themselves increasingly with their peers as a means of judging success (Ruble et al., 1994). However, the most influential input comes from parents and carers: how they use praise and rewards, and how they explain and provide clear and consistent rules (Hughes, 2002). Carers and parents who expect the best from their children tend to have children who give of their best: children who are thought well of , learn that they should think well of themselves. Where parents have reasonable expectations for mature behaviour and are warm and accepting they help to nurture children who feel good about themselves (Carolson, Uppal and Prosser, 2000; Feiring and Taska, 1996). It is important for us to encourage parents and carers in this process and to help them to understand their role in building the self-confidence of their child.

Practical tasks

Provide an opportunity for children to set up an activity and to clear away at its end. Monitor the contribution made by different children, levels of cooperation and whether children participate in isolation or offer help to one another.

- Evaluate the contribution made by each child.
- Did the children gain a sense of pride from being responsible for their own resources?
- How could you provide structure or support to promote positive attitudes and independence?
- What opportunities can you create to promote further independence and personal responsibility?

Conclusion

This chapter has explored some of the ways in which children's dispositions and attitudes can be nurtured in order to lay a positive foundation on which to build future learning and relationships. These areas relate particularly to the need, identified in the outcomes of the Every Child Matters agenda (DfES, 2004) to be healthy (particularly to foster positive mental health), enjoy and achieve and make a positive contribution.

Every child is a unique individual with their own characteristics and temperament. Although some aspects of temperament may be inherited, the ways in which children are nurtured and supported can help them to develop positive dispositions towards others. As children grow, the complex interaction between genetic and environmental factors requires that professionals monitor carefully a child's development and provide both support and positive role models. Early relationships have a particularly strong impact on how children develop and the ways in which we support parents/carers and develop relationships ourselves with children is key to making sure they have the most supported experience possible.

Understanding that they are special, unique and precious is fundamental to building a child's self-identity and self-esteem and to fostering positive dispositions and attitudes. Learning to care, share, be honest, respectful and independent are all positive facets of personality that support a confident and enjoyable experience of life. As professionals we are in the privileged position of being able to help lay such a foundation.

References

Ainsworth, M. D. S., Blehar, M. C., Waters, E. and Wall, S. (1978) *Patterns of Attachment: A Psychological Study of the Strange Situation.* Hillsdale, NJ: Erlbaum

Astington, J. W. (1993) *The Child's Discovery of the Mind.* Cambridge, MA: Harvard University Press

Bee, H. and Boyd, D. (2003) *The Developing Child* (10th edition). Boston, MA: Allyn and Bacon.

Berger, K. (2000) *The Developing Person: Through Childhood* (2nd edition). New York: Worth Publishers

Berk, L. (2006) *Child Development* (7th edition). Boston, MA: Pearson Education

Bowlby, J. (1951) *Maternal Care and Mental Health.* World Health Organisation Monograph (Serial No 2)

Brooker, Liz and Broadbent, Lynne (2003) 'Personal, social and emotional development: The child makes meaning in a social world', in J. Riley (ed.) *Learning in the Early Years; a Guide for Teachers of Children 3–7.* London: Paul Chapman Publishing

Carolson, C., Uppal, S. and Prosser, E. (2000) 'Ethnic differences in processes contributing to the self-esteem of early adolescent girls'. *Journal of Early Adolescence,* 20, 44–67

DCSF (2008a) *Statutory Framework for the Early Years Foundation Stage.* London: Department for Children, Schools and Families

DCSF (2008b) *Practice Guidance for the Early Years Foundation Stage.* London: Department for Children, Schools and Families

DeHart, G., Sroufe, L. and Cooper, R. (2004) *Child Development: Its Nature and Course* (5th edition). Boston, MA: McGraw Hill

DfES (2004) *Every Child Matters: Change for Children in Schools.* London: Department for Education and Skills

Digman, J. M. (1990) 'Personality structure: Emergence of the five-factor model'. *Annual Review of Psychology,* 41, 417–440

Einon, D. (2001) *Dorothy Einon's Complete Book of Childcare and Development: Raising Happy, Health and Confident Children.* London: Marshall Publishing

Eisenberg, N. (1988) 'The development of prosocial and aggressive behaviour', in M. H. Borstein and M. E. Lamb (eds) *Developmental Psychology: An Advanced Textbook* (2nd edition). Hillsdale, NJ: Erlbaum, pp. 461–496

Eisenberg, N. and Fabes, R. (1998) 'Prosocial development', in W. Damon (series ed.) and N. Eisenberg (vol. ed.) *Handbook of Child Psychology*. Vol. 3, *Social Emotional and Personality Development* (5th edition). New York: Wiley, pp. 701–778

Feiring, C. and Taska, L. S. (1996) 'Family self-concept: Ideas on its meaning', in B. Bracken (ed.) *Handbook of Self-concept*. New York: Wiley, pp. 317–373

Freedman, D. G. and Freedman, N. (1969) 'Behavioural differences between Chinese-American and European newborns'. *Nature*, 224, 1227

Grossman, K., Grossman, K. E., Spangler, G., Suess, G. and Unzer, L. (1985) 'Maternal sensitivity and newborns' orientation responses as related to quality of attachment in Northern Germany', in I. Bretherton and E. Waters (eds) Growing points of attachment theory and research. Monographs of the Society for Research in Child Development, 50 (1–2, Serial No. 209)

Heyman, G. D. and Gelman, S. A. (1999) 'The use of trait labels in making psychological inferences'. *Child Development*, 70, 604–619

Hohmann, M. and Weikart, D. P. (2002) *Educating Young Children* (2nd edition). Ypsilanti, MI: High/Scope Press

Hughes, L. (2002) *Paving Pathways: Child and Adolescent Development*. Belmont, CA: Wadsworth

Kagan, J. (1992) 'Yesterday's Premises, Tomorrow's Promises'. *Developmental Psychology*, 28, 990–997

Lewis, M. and Brooks-Gunn, J. (1979) *Social Cognition and the Acquisition of the Self*. New York: Plenum Press

Main, M. and Solomon, J. (1990) 'Procedures for identifying infants as disorganized/disoriented during the Ainsworth Strange Situation', in M. T. Greenberg, D. Cicchetti and E. M. Cummings (eds) *Attachment in the Preschool Years: Theory, Research, and Intervention*. Chicago: University of Chicago Press

McCrae, R., Costa, P., de Lima, M., Simoes, A., Ostendorf, F., Angleitner, A., Marusic, I., Bratko, D., Caprara, G., Barbaranelli, C., Chae, J. and Piedmont, R. (1999) 'Age differences in personality across the adult life span: Parallels in five cultures'. *Developmental Psychology*, 35, 466–477

McDonald, K. B. (1995) 'Evolution, the five-factor model, and levels of personality'. *Journal of Personality*, 63(3) 525–567

Miyake, K., Chen, S. and Campos, J. J. (1985) 'Infant temperament, mother's mode of interaction and attachment in Japan: An interim report'. Monographs of the Society for Research in Child Development, 50, 276–297

Papalia, D., Gross, D. and Feldman, R. (2003) *Child Development: A Topical Approach*. New York: McGraw Hill

Premack, D. and Woodruff, G. (1978) 'Does the chimpanzee have a theory of mind?'. *The Behavioural and Brain Sciences*, 1, 515–526

Puckett, M. and Black, J. (2001) *The Young Child: Development from Prebirth through Age Eight* (3rd edition). Upper Saddle River, NJ: Prentice Hall

Rothbart, M. K. and Bates, J. E. (1998) 'Temperament', in W. Damon (series ed.) and N. Eisenberg (vol. ed.) *Handbook of Child Psychology*. Vol. 3, *Social Emotional and Personality Development* (5th edition). New York: Wiley, pp. 105–176

Rubin, K., Burgess, K. and Hastings, P. (2002) 'Stability and social-behavioural consequences of toddlers' inhibited temperament and parenting behaviors'. *Child Development*, 73, 483–495

Ruble, D. N., Eisenberg, R. and Higgins, E. T. (1994) 'Developmental changes in achievement evaluations: Motivational implications of self-other differences'. *Child Development*, 65, 1095–1110

Santrock, J. (2007) *Child Development* (11th edition). New York: McGraw Hill

Smith, P., Cowie, H. and Blades, M. (2003) *Understanding Children's Development* (4th edition). Malden, MA: Blackwell Publishing

Takahashi, K. (1990) 'Are the key assumptions of the "Strange Situation" procedure universal? A view from Japanese research'. *Human Development*, 33, 23–30

Self-Confidence and Self-Esteem

2

Introduction

A sense of self is a fundamental aspect of being human. We define ourselves in a range of ways through the relationships we share and the activities in which we engage: we may be a child, a parent, a plumber or a teacher, a dancer or a footballer. Relating to others and knowing that our words, actions and thoughts are valued is an essential part of developing self-confidence and positive self-esteem. Implicit to this is the need to develop a sense of self-respect, to show respect to others and to understand that we should, ourselves, be respected.

This chapter explores how children learn to relate to others in cooperative and collaborative ways, developing an understanding of fairness and appreciating the benefits of harmonious relationships. Central to this is the knowledge that it is positive to try something new but not achieve immediate success, and that exploring new ideas is good even if the 'right' answer is not found. Establishing good relationships is a fundamental part of developing the confidence to learn and grow, both in terms of knowledge and emotion. This chapter considers how children can be enabled to share their feelings so that they are able to deal with success and elation, frustration and 'failure'. Examples will be used to consider strategies to use with children who have a range of skills and confidence levels. In addition, ways of working with parents and carers to help to promote children's self-confidence and self-esteem are outlined. It is important to acknowledge that, despite the existence of different theoretical models and patters of child development, all children are unique and develop at their own pace. The chapter considers how to value such growth and learning in order to value difference and diversity.

Understanding the concepts of self-confidence and self-esteem

A general term for how people think about themselves is self-concept, or identity. This relates to a breadth of aspects of the self: personality, ability, appearance, gender and social or cultural group. Some aspects of one's identity are evaluative as we all compare ourselves to others and think that we are good at some things and not so good at others (Smith, Cowie and Blades, 2003; Dowling, 2005). Psychologists term these evaluations self-esteem.

A personal example may serve to illustrate the point. I know that I am not a very good pianist and I do not like to perform in front of anyone. I used to play in the assembly at school and for the Christmas pantomime, but I have not practised a great deal since I was a student. If someone tells me how good I am, I find it difficult to accept the compliment because I know that I do not play as well as I used to and I cannot play to a standard that I feel particularly proud of. To some people I am a good pianist – probably because I can play a song or a piece of music far better than they can. But to myself I am not very good at all – because I know that I used to be much better and that there are many more people with greater talent and competence. Thus, my self-esteem in this area is quite low: I make an evaluation of myself based on my own expectations, perceptions and wider knowledge. Whatever other people say makes little difference.

We have all worked with children who have varying levels of confidence and will have come across children who are able but who do not evaluate their abilities positively. We are all well aware that children thrive when their emotional needs are being met and that they fail to thrive when emotional support and care is absent. Confidence brings the opportunity to try new things and to gain success. When we achieve and experience such success it spurs us on to attempt new things and to achieve further successes. In any learning setting it is important to ensure that our objectives are realistic so that they move a child forward in their learning without over-facing them with tasks or activities which will lead to a sense of failure. As professionals, our aim is to provide children with a range of experiences and to share praise and positive feelings when they show a willingness to try and when they achieve success. We need to help to make the next steps manageable and to encourage children to appreciate that they are progressing. By celebrating their successes we hope to help them to find pleasure in learning so that they enjoy it and grow in their positive evaluation of themselves.

It is important to remember that self-confident people may not be confident in every aspect of their lives. We may be confident academically but not on the sports field, or vice versa; we may be confident in our social skills but not with our personal appearance. However, a confident person may have a sense of control over their own life that enables them to plan and do much of what they wish within their own realistic expectations. Even if such expectations are not met they have the resilience to deal with this, to maintain a positive outlook and to accept themselves. Those with self-confidence do not necessarily feel the need to conform, as they accept themselves as they are and do not feel the need to please others or conform to their expectations in order to be accepted.

Self-confidence and ability

It is important to consider the dual concepts of self-confidence and ability. The two are not necessarily related or interlinked. Some people find it difficult to accept compliments, some notice single failures despite having had several successes and others feel that if they have not pleased everybody then they have pleased no one. Being able to appraise and appreciate one's own success is an important part of developing self-confidence as it internalizes positive thoughts, which might be dismissed if offered by others. Thus developing effective skills of self-evaluation and self-assessment are key to building self-confidence and self-esteem. Dowling (2005) suggests that children do not gain a clear view of their self-worth until around the age of 6 years. However, their experience in the family and in early years settings provides the basis for them to make judgements about themselves from an earlier age.

Self-confidence and self-esteem from birth to 3 years of age

From birth children are interested in interacting with the people around them. They are particularly engaged when talk involves them and is directed towards them. This attention gives an early sense of self-esteem and of being valued and helps to develop secure attachments to special people including parents, carers and family members (Hughes, 2002; Dunn 1993). The concept of attachment was introduced in Chapter 1. These individuals are able to begin to develop a child's sense of self-confidence by providing quality experiences that engage all the senses.

From the ages of 8–20 months the provision of a quality environment that is safe and stimulating helps children to develop curiosity and to gain the confidence to explore, develop coordination and develop further their physical abilities. A child's developing communication skills mean that they can express their needs and feelings and begin to develop a sense of self (DCSF, 2008a; 2008b). They are aware of the tastes and smells that they like and are engaged by sounds, shapes and colours. Having a range of attractive and colourful toys with varied textures provides an array of sensory, stimulating and enjoyable experiences. At this age children express pleasure in a sense of achievement and begin to be sensitive to adult evaluations of their actions (Berk, 2006).

From 16–26 months children need to experience a range of activities that reflect their increasing physical strengths and also quieter times for calm activities. Playing with other children provides an opportunity to develop interaction and self-confidence. During this phase children are also learning to deal with frustration and to understand boundaries. Throughout this time adults provide an essential source of comfort and security and play a key role in developing children's self-esteem and confidence. A young child will often use their parent or carer as a base from which to explore wider territory, referring to their parent when they meet new people to see if they are safe to interact with (Sylva and Lunt, 1982). In the same way that children need physical and sensory stimulation to promote normal body and brain growth, they also need social stimulation to support their emotional and social development (Hughes, 2002).

From 22 months to the age of 3 years children are developing their literacy skills by making marks, using various materials and enjoying picture books. This can provide a great sense of achievement that nurtures self-esteem and gives a sense of 'growing up' and taking on greater independence. This independence if evidenced further through dressing, toileting and feeding themselves. Self-esteem is built through praise for such new achievements. In addition, the development of verbal communication means that children can increasingly join in conversations and talk about the past, present and future (DCSF, 2008a; 2008b). Such engagement gives a sense that their ideas are valued and valuable and by trying out an increasing vocabulary a sense of achievement is gained.

By 36 months most children can correctly label their own, or another person's, sex or gender and are said to have achieved gender identity (Smith, Cowie and Blades, 2003). This is followed by gender stability (at around 4 years) when children understand that gender is normally stable, and gender constancy (by around 7 years) when they realize that biological sex is unchanging, despite changes in appearance (Papalia, Gross and Feldman, 2003). Gender will play an important part in a child's sense of self as they mature; having security in their gender identity as a part of their overall sense of self will help to give them the confidence to be themselves. Williams and Best (1990) found that boys are expected to show instrumental traits (e.g. competitiveness and assertiveness) and girls are expected to show more expressive traits (e.g. care, sensitivity and being considerate) in over 30 different countries. As professionals, we need to be aware of those who do not conform to traditional gender roles or stereotypes, as this is a common cause of bullying which can crush self-esteem (DfES, 2000; DCSF, 2007). We need to consider how to get beyond such stereotypes so that children can be themselves without restriction and we need to challenge stereotyping when it occurs.

Case study

David is aged 26 months. He enjoys indoor play and crawls under furniture and climbs on chairs; he enjoys the different levels available in the living room and in his bedroom. He particularly likes to hide and finds it hilarious when an adult comes to 'find' him. With his older brother's help he likes to climb on the back of the sofa and crawl along the top of the cushions (although his mum does not approve of this). When I observed David it was clear that he had a great deal of energy and found delight in using the furniture as a 'mini assault course'. However, when I visited again on a warm spring afternoon I found David and his mum in the garden. David was constructing a wall from wooden bricks, and would periodically knock the wall over, laugh and reconstruct it. He showed no interest in running around the garden, hiding in the bushes or shrubs or playing on his slide. His mother expressed her concern that he is apparently confident and boisterous indoors, but lacks confidence and a willingness to explore when outdoors.

Photograph 2.1 Children playing in the playground (© P. Hopkins)

Reflection for early career professional

- Why might David show greater confidence when playing indoors?
- What activities would you devise and what support could you give to help him to explore the outdoor environment?
- What strategies might help to boost David's confidence in the outdoor environment and how might you nurture his self-esteem?

Reflection for leader/manager

- Do you encourage colleagues to evaluate children's development and skills in a range of environments to focus on their achievement rather than their location?
- How do you promote an incremental approach to introduce children gradually to new environments and experiences, as appropriate for their needs?
- How do health and safety considerations support confidence building and how do they mitigate against appropriate risk-taking/discovery by children?

Self-confidence and self-esteem from 3 to 5 years of age

From the age of 30–50 months children enjoy a growing interest in cooperative play and are able to help adults with daily tasks in the home. They begin to find a balance between going along with the wishes of others and finding their own independence. During this phase it is important to find comfort from special people in the child's life and the sense of security that this brings (DCSF, 2008a). Children begin to form a sense of self and others on the basis of age, gender, physical characteristics, competencies and goodness/badness (Berk, 2006).

From 40 months to the age of 5 years children have a much stronger sense of their own identity and are beginning to find their place in the wider world. Their view of themselves is all-or-none, with the real self thought to be the same as the ideal self (Papalia, Gross and Feldman, 2003). This makes it important of us to make sure that children have opportunities to succeed and that they do not damage their self-esteem by setting themselves unmanageable goals and activities and thus becoming frustrated. They are now better able to plan and undertake a wider range of activities that involve making, doing and problem-solving and to face greater challenges. The praise that this can bring for attempting new activities and for achieving success is important in building both self-confidence and self-esteem.

During this phase, entering an early years setting can be a momentous experience for a child. We may think of our own experiences of starting a new job or commencing a new course of study, but a child has less life experience on which to draw for support in that situation. Dowling (2005) notes that even the most confident child can find this move intimidating: the setting plays an important role in managing the transition from the home and in maintaining the child's self-esteem when they are learning to work and play in a new environment. It is helpful that children's self-esteem is usually high at the age when they begin formal education (Bukatko and Daehler, 2004) and we can draw upon this to help them to face new challenges, relationships and environments.

Case study

In one piece of research with four reception children, aged 5 years old, I shared a range of untuned percussion instruments during a music activity and asked them to explore what sounds could be made. After a time when they could explore independently in a relatively unstructured way we came together to talk about each instrument and to show and share what we had discovered.

Observing the unstructured part of the activity I could see that two of the children were more confident in exploring freely. Jackie and Ian scraped, shook, banged and tapped the instruments, and at one point Jackie started to combine instruments to see what sounds they made when they collided. Alan and Duncan were more cautious. Initially Alan watched Jane and then began to make sounds using ideas he had gained from his observation. Duncan chose to play a pair of claves, but did not explore the other instruments. Jackie was keen to show the others her discoveries saying, 'Look at this!' 'Have you tried doing this?' and 'I think this one sounds great.'

I asked the children to explain the sounds that they had discovered during the unstructured part of the activity. Their respective responses suggest varying degrees of familiarity with the instruments and confidence:

Richard: *Who would like to play me a sound they really liked?*
Jackie: *I scraped this [the guiro] against this one [a cymbal] and it made a tingly noise that made me feel all funny inside.*
Ian: *That's not how you play a cymbal, you should hit it hard and make it wobble!*
Jackie: *But it's more fun if you do two things.*
Ian: *But you have to do it properly and make it . . . crash.*
Alan: *I liked the metal [cymbal] and the scraper. The sound went inside me.*

Richard: *Ian, have you seen people play the cymbal before?*

Ian: *I have seen it on the TV and you have to hit it hard to make a bang.*

Richard: *Did you like the new sound that Jackie made?*

Ian: *It was scary but it's not meant to be like that. You are meant to do it like this [scraping the guiro with a beater]. You have got to do it right.*

Jackie: *I can do it properly but I like scraping the cymbal.*

Richard: *Duncan, what sound did you like best?*

Duncan: *I like the wooden sticks [claves] because they sound like a horse running or I can make them like a clock [ticking]. I know how to do them. But it's not a song . . . I like it better when you play a piano or a guitar and do a tune . . . at home I can make up tunes on my own when no one is listening and do concerts for myself.*

Ian: *You can't play a tune with these . . . they just bang . . . it's the same sound all the time.*

Alan: *You can do a tune but it doesn't go up and down it all sounds the same.*

Jackie: But we weren't trying to play tunes we were making noises . . . it was like an experiment. We were finding out.

Reflection for early career professional

- How do the children's different responses show different levels of confidence, knowledge and experience?
- What questions or interactions do you think would support further exploration and encourage more confident investigation?
- How would you respond to each child to develop their self-confidence and self-esteem?

Reflection for leader/manager

- Review the activities you provide in your setting. How do they enable the children to develop self-confidence and willingness to investigate and discover?
- How do you enable children to develop confidence through a range of sensory experiences? Is there a greater focus on some senses or skills than on others in your setting?
- How do you value experience from outside the setting (e.g. the home) so that positive self-esteem and self-confidence from one environment is transferred to another?

Transition to Key Stage 1 (5 to 7 years of age)

The transition from the Early Years Foundation Stage to Key Stage 1 brings significant change. The more formal style of learning associated with Key Stage 1 can involve increased time sitting and listening to the teacher, more formal literacy and numeracy lessons and less opportunity for self-directed activity. For some children this brings a sense of progression and growth, but it can also bring frustration and limit creative opportunities for self-directed learning.

Creative approaches to the Key Stage 1 curriculum build on the Early Learning Goals and the curriculum for the Early Years Foundation Stage. It is important to maintain the focus on developing personal, social and emotional education and knowledge and understanding of the world while also introducing the more traditional subject-based curriculum. It was positive that the report of the *Rose Review* (DCSF, 2009) encouraged such approaches and a move towards a more integrated curriculum model. It is essential to maintain a skills-based curriculum alongside a focus on knowledge-based learning. Maintaining self-esteem is important and requires a sensitive transition to different pedagogical approaches. Schools have a degree of flexibility about how they structure the learning environment and how they deliver the curriculum. This provides the opportunity to ensure continuity between different learning environments and, indeed, to maintain the ethos of the foundation stage into Year 1 and beyond if the school so chooses.

In some schools a decision is made that the EYFS teacher should progress with the children into Key Stage 1. This provides the opportunity to ensure continuity and to build upon the effective relationships already established with both children and parents and carers. It also allows for seamless continuity in the assessment of children and in the gradual adaptation to the new learning environment. All of this can play an important part in maintaining children's self-confidence and ensuring that they feel safe and secure in their relationships with professionals. It can also remove some of the anxiety faced by parents and carers during such a move. Research suggests that children approach such transitions with resilience and enjoy the rite of passage, with only limited apprehensions (Ofsted, 2004). Although this approach to transition is not common, it does suggest elements of continuity that are important for us to consider as children move from one class or setting to another and challenges us to strive for continuity as well as progression.

Case study

Sam', Lee and Chris' have been friends since before they entered nursery. They are all 6 years of age and are in the same class at school. They play together during break times and meet up regularly after school as they live in the same street. When they play or learn together they are talkative and lively and appear very confident. However, if they have to work in different groups for literacy or numeracy activities they appear much quieter and need a great deal of encouragement to offer answers or to share ideas.

Reflection for early career professional

- How would you support the children to help them to develop confidence when working away from their friends?
- What benefits and drawbacks can you identify from allowing this group to work together on activities?
- Did you visualize the children as a group of boys or girls, or a mixed group? Would your approach differ if you changed this assumption?

Reflection for leader/manager

- What approaches do you have in your setting to the use of friendship groups when organizing activities?
- Do you encourage colleagues to adapt and rearrange groups for different activities?
- Analyse how you and your colleagues group children. If it is by ability, how is a child's ability in different learning/curriculum areas identified and monitored? If it is by friendship group, how do children encounter new relationships and learn to cooperate with a variety of children from different backgrounds?

Promoting children's health and well-being

The DfEE (2001) suggests that there are important characteristics shared by Early Years settings which promote the emotional well-being of children. These include stable childcare arrangements that enable children to work with just a few primary caregivers in any one day; effective use of behaviour management techniques; low staff turnover that enables effective long-term relationships to be established with children and parents/carers; the levels of staff training; and child-staff ratios. All this is augmented and supported by the provision of an effective curriculum that aims to do more than instil knowledge and is concerned with the development of the whole child. Indeed, early childhood education may be viewed as an effective strategy that affects many risk and protective factors relating to a child's mental health and well-being (Weissberg, Caplan and Harwood, 1991).

Photograph 2.2 Children working cooperatively (Photography by L. Nahmad-Williams)

The *Statutory Framework for the Early Years Foundation Stage* (DCSF, 2008a) has set out key principles for early years practitioners in relation to children's personal, social and emotional development. I identify key elements from the

Early Learning Goals (DCSF, 2008a: 12) that are particularly relevant to this chapter as being to:

- *be confident to try new activities, initiate ideas and speak in a familiar group;*
- *respond to significant experiences, showing a range of feelings when appropriate;*
- *form good relationships with adults and peers;*
- *work as a part of a group or class, taking turns and sharing fairly, understanding that their needs to be agreed values and codes of behaviour for groups of people, including adults and children, to work together harmoniously;*
- *dress and undress independently and manage their own personal hygiene;*
- *select and use activities and resources independently;*
- *understand that they can expect others to treat their needs, views and cultures and beliefs with respect.*

Those of us working with younger children will identify the elements relevant to our own professional setting and appropriate to the needs and development of the children in our care. Additionally, those working in Key Stage 1 need to maintain an awareness of the development and achievements that have already been attained and to consider how the themes and content of the learning goals can impact upon the themes and threads in their own curriculum programmes.

Among other important issues, the DfEE (2001:8) highlights that practitioners should give special attention to:

- *establishing constructive relationships with children, with other practitioners, between practitioners and children, with parents and with workers from other agencies, that take account of differences and different needs and expectations;*
- *planning activities that promote emotional, moral, spiritual and social development alongside intellectual development;*
- *providing support and a structured approach to achieve the successful social and emotional development of vulnerable children and those with particular behavioural and communication difficulties.*

Furthermore, the DfEE (2001: 15) states that research has shown the important role that early years practitioners can play, 'in assisting parents to recognize when their child may be experiencing difficulties outside of the norm, to help them and the child address some of the problems they may be experiencing and where appropriate refer them on to more specialist help'. Our role as professionals is important in nurturing children's confidence, self-esteem, well-being and mental health. These aspects of life are intertwined and contribute to a positive sense of self-identity which enables children to learn and grow into confident and self-assured young people and adults.

Studies suggest that children develop most effectively when they are provided with opportunities to direct and evaluate their own learning. Where professionals use open-ended questions to allow children to develop their own answers, where they allow children to make decisions and where activities arise from a genuine interest children are enabled to develop more satisfying social and personal lives (Dowling, 2005).

Considering issues beyond the setting

There are many issues outside our setting that impact on a child's self-esteem and sense of self-worth. They may also affect their physical or mental health and development. Examples include:

- Housing
- Diet
- Unemployment
- Availability of learning resources in the home and the community
- Parental confidence and self-esteem
- The availability of safe outdoor and green spaces for play
- Health needs

Many of these relate to Maslow's hierarchy of needs (1968) and have a significant impact on readiness and capacity to learn. While several will be beyond our control as practitioners, we need to ensure that our settings provide safe, warm, supportive and stimulating environments that can compensate for any deficit outside the setting and nurture children's self-esteem as much as possible. It is also important that we do not make judgements based on these needs that cause us to under-estimate the capabilities of our children, otherwise we will become a part of any problem rather than part of the solution.

I have seen good practice in many settings that helps to address some of the needs found in local communities, which include:

- setting up a community room where parents and carers can meet, drink coffee, share conversation and find a warm, safe place;
- organizing a toy library, using items donated as children grow up, so that learners can borrow a variety of resources to use at home;
- a clothing store, using items which children have outgrown and which are not needed by families anymore and distributed freely according to need or sold for a small cost;
- running short courses or advice sessions for parents and carers to help them to support their child's learning or to develop their own skills (e.g. in IT or literacy);
- making space available in the setting for visits by health professionals, the local college or learning/employment advisors;
- organizing social occasions to bring members of the community together and to help make the setting accessible and welcoming to parents and carers (e.g. Bingo, coffee mornings, cookery demonstrations).

I have heard professionals suggest that some of these activities are beyond the role or remit of their setting. Clearly not all will be appropriate in every setting. However, if we are to address the needs of the whole child, and to maximize opportunities for growth and learning, we need to be imaginative and creative in exploring ways to help families so that children are ready to learn.

Practical tasks

Choose two strategies used in your setting to provide praise and affirmation. Focus on their use during one session and:

- evaluate how effective each one was in boosting self-esteem;
- which was most effective, and why?
- did some children respond better to one strategy than to the other? Why might this be?
- consider whether age, gender or ability were factors in the effectiveness of the strategies.

Providing stimulating experiences for growth and learning

Three of the outcomes of Every Child Matters (DfES, 2004) relate directly to the development of self-confidence and self-esteem, to:

- be healthy,
- enjoy and achieve, and
- make a positive contribution.

A child with positive self-esteem is more lively to have an optimistic outlook on life which, in turn, helps them to enjoy and achieve. Their level of happiness will be higher which impacts on their mental health and well-being. This brings greater resilience and an increased capacity to face the challenges of life. As practitioners we face the challenge of designing activities that enable children to face the next steps in their growth and learning in ways which address these areas.

One approach that has become increasingly common in learning settings is the use of circle time. White (1991; 2008) describes the benefits of the circle time approach to raising self-esteem, in which children discuss the positive views of others and give advice about how to face personal difficulties. He sees this as being particularly effective as it is a way of gaining positive feedback from both peers and professionals. Taking the time to give such affirmation, and to explore strategies so that the children have a wider range of options when they face challenges, can pay great dividends. While teachers sometimes speak of the curriculum being over-crowded and pressured, the benefits of taking time to nurture children's sense of self through circle time helps them to approach other aspects of their time in the setting with greater confidence and independence, which makes the time spent worthwhile and productive.

It is also important for use to consider the different ways in which children learn, to cater for these interests in the activities we plan and to help children become familiar and confident with other ways of learning. In past years teachers have been considering children's learning styles. This led some to label children in different ways, for example as visual, auditory or kinaesthetic learners. While an understanding of the ways in which children learn can help us to support their development, such labels can be unhelpful and limiting: we each learn through all three ways although we may have a preference for one or another. It is important for us to help children to learn through the means that they find most useful and effective but also for use to help them to develop other facets or approaches to learning so that they have an increasingly wide range of experience and expertise on which to draw.

Practical tasks

Plan and set up an outdoor play activity for the children in your care.
Evaluate the activity and identify what it revealed about:

- the self-confidence of individual children;
- confidence in interacting with other children;
- each child's use of space and their creativity/imagination.

Repeat the process for a cognitive task with the same group. How do your observations differ? How might this inform your practice and the ways in which you meet the needs of the child in a holistic manner?

Supporting parents and carers

Some children do not have a perception of themselves as learners when they enter an early years setting. Parents or carers may have been over-protective and have not allowed children to make mistakes or to discover by trying things out for themselves. Adults may have disregarded some children's thoughts and views. This will have communicated the message that the child is not able to do things for themselves and that they are not important. These children may require a great deal of support and reassurance from professionals and may tend to give up easily when faced with new activities. Other children will have what Dowling (2005) calls mastery patterns of behaviour: they are confident and willing to try and grasp new skills.

While children and parents/carers may have many established behaviour patterns by the time a child enters our setting, we can support them to promote learning and development by:

- using everyday experiences to generate genuine interest in finding out;
- learning to ask open questions that do not have a prescribed or expected answer;

- listening carefully to their child and showing that what is said is appreciated and interesting;
- sharing thoughts, ideas and feelings with their child to model being engaged and excited by situations and experiences;
- allowing children to try new things for themselves, with appropriate support or supervision, and praising effort as well as success;
- telling the child that they are special and reinforcing this by identifying specific attributes and skills shown by the child.

Montessori (1936) told the story of a nurse who pushed a child aged 5 months in her carriage (pushchair) each day. She stopped according to the child's spontaneous interest in the world around her and noted the girl's particular interests in aspects of the environment. Similarly, Crain (2005) suggests that parents who follow their child as they learn to walk, stop when they stop and allow them to find interesting new sights provide a valuable learning opportunity. In contrast, some parents/carers limit opportunities to learn to walk by using playpens, or presume that the purpose of walking is to reach a destination and so pick up the child or place them in a push chair in order to reach somewhere with greater speed. While this may be realistic and practical in some instances, being a follower, rather than the director, of a child's interests is very much in the Montessori tradition of encouraging independence and enthusiasm for learning. Sometimes it is the journey – rather than the destination – that provides the greatest opportunities for learning.

Engaging parents and carers can be a slow, and sometimes frustrating, process. However the medium to long-term benefits can be worth the effort involved. Given that the parent/carer is the child's primary educator it is essential to take steps to engage them as partners in our setting.

Conclusion

Self-confidence is not an all-encompassing part of a person's life. We are all confident in some areas and less so in others. However, confidence in ourselves supports the skills and attributes necessary to face a lack of success or a weakness in a particular area. Being self-assured in some or many aspects of life impinges on other areas and helps to bring about a positive sense of self-esteem. Being aware of some of the pressures faced by children, particularly during times of transition, helps us as professionals to provide safe and secure environments in which children can flourish. An understanding and awareness of mental health issues helps us to appreciate one dimension of children's experience that, in turn, helps us to nurture the whole child. While self-esteem is difficult to measure (Miell, 1995) it is important that we regularly consider it as an important aspect of a child's development.

The degree of match between children's aspirations and their performance is important in determining feelings of self-esteem. We need to be aware of those children who have unrealistic expectation of themselves and who may repeatedly be setting themselves up to fail. Similarly, we need to help children who are too easily pleased with their own efforts to expect the best from themselves and to seek to learn new skills and try new techniques and activities.

The respect given to children by significant others, including professionals, peers and parents/carers is an important factor in determining self-esteem. While self-esteem is based to a significant degree on the ways in which we evaluate ourselves, we can help children to find a belief in themselves through the messages that we communicate to them. This can be particularly challenging for us as professionals when children enter our setting with low self-esteem having received little praise, attention or affirmation in the home. However, the opportunity to begin to address this is one of the privileges, and challenges, of working in an educational setting and, as we know, brings tremendous rewards when we are successful.

References

Berk, L. (2006) *Child Development* (7th edition). Boston, MA: Pearson Education

Bukatko, D. and Daehler, M. (2004) *Child Development: A Thematic Approach* (5th edition). Boston, MA: Houghton Mifflin Company

Crain, W. (2005) *Theories of Development: Concepts and Applications.* London: Prentice Hall

DCSF (2007) *Safe to Learn: Embedding Anti-bullying Work in Schools.* London: Department for Children, Schools and Families

DCSF (2008a) *Statutory Framework for the Early Years Foundation Stage.* London: Department for Children, Schools and Families

DCSF (2008b) *Practice Guidance for the Early Years Foundation Stage.* London: Department for Children, Schools and Families

DCSF (2009) *Independent Review of the Primary Curriculum: Final Report* (the Rose Review). DCSF: London

DfEE (2001) *Promoting Children's Mental Health in Early Years and School Settings.* London: Department for Education and Employment

DfES (2000) *Bullying: Don't Suffer in Silence.* London: Department for Education and Skills

DfES (2004) *Every Child Matters: Change for Children in Schools*. London: Department for Education and Skills

Dowling, M. (2005) *Young Children's Personal, Social and Emotional Development* (2nd edition). London: Paul Chapman Publishing

Dunn, J. (1993) *Young Children's Close Relationships beyond Attachment*. Individual Differences and Development Series, Vol. 4. Newbury Park, CA: Sage

Hughes, L. (2002) *Paving Pathways: Child and Adolescent Development*. Belmont, CA: Wadsworth

Maslow, A. (1968) *Towards a Psychology of Being* (2nd edition). New York: D. Van Nostrand Co

Miell, D. (1995) 'Developing a sense of self', in P. Barnes (ed.) *Personal, Social and Emotional Development of Children*. Oxford: Blackwell Publishers

Montessori, M. (1936) *The Secret of Childhood*. London: Longmans Green & Co

Ofsted (2004) *Transition from the Reception Year to Year 1: An Evaluation by HMI* (HMI 2221). London: Office for Standards in Education

Papalia, D., Gross, D. and Feldman, R. (2003) *Child Development: A Topical Approach*. New York: McGraw Hill

Smith, P., Cowie, H. and Blades, M. (2003) *Understanding Children's Development* (4th edition). Malden, MA: Blackwell Publishing

Sylva, K. and Lunt, I. (1982) *Child Development: A First Course*. Oxford: Blackwell

Weissberg, R., Caplan, M. and Harwood, R. (1991) 'Promoting competent young people in competence enhancing environments: A systems-based perspective on primary prevention'. *Journal of Consulting and Clinical Psychology*, 59, 830–841

White, M. (1991) *Self-esteem – its Meaning and Value in Schools: How to Help Children Learn Readily and Behave Well*. Cambridge: Daniels

White, M. (2008) *Magic Circles: Self-esteem for Everyone through Circle Time*. London: Sage

Williams, J. E. and Best, D. L. (1990) *Measuring Sex Stereotypes: A Multi-nation Study*. Newbury Park, CA: Sage

Making Relationships

3

Chapter Outline

Introduction

I have been researching children's play in early years settings for over 20 years. Much of this research has been undertaken jointly with early years practitioners. We have observed children's play with peers, recorded our observations and reflected together on what we have learned about children's interests and pre-occupations, on the benefits of play and on the links between play and children's learning. I will draw on some of these observations in this chapter to illustrate how children make relationships in their early years setting and how adults can help to facilitate the making and sustaining of these important relationships with their peers and with adults. I also want to illustrate how good relationships are linked to being motivated to learn in early years settings. The Practice Guidance for the EYFS tells us (p. 22): '*Children must be provided with experiences and support which will help them to develop a positive sense of themselves and of others; respect for others; social skills, and a positive disposition to learn. Providers must ensure support for children's well-being to help them to know themselves and what they can do.'* But what does this mean in practice? The following chapter aims to unpack this a little in relation to play and playful learning.

My research has always focussed on three research questions:

- What potential do traditional activities have for supporting the development of cooperation in children in educational settings?
- What range of sociable and cooperative behaviours are children exhibiting and using across the age range?
- How do these behaviours inter-connect in facilitating intellectual commitment and supporting learning?

The link between this research and the focus of this chapter is that the observations have always focused on children's engagements with their peers in the sand, water, large and small construction, role play, small world and more recently on open-ended role play or the 'whatever you want it to be place' as it came to be called (Broadhead 1997; 2001; 2004). Apart from the last area, that came directly out of the research (Broadhead, 2004), these other activities or areas are what I would term the 'traditional activities' of question 1 – places where previous research has shown, children would gather together and begin to interact with their peers in quite natural but increasingly complex ways as they became older and more familiar with the settings and the resources available to them. It was from these interactions I was able to study the sociable and cooperative engagements that the children initiated with one another and that I would also be able to connect with learning to address that elusive question – what are children learning when they play together?

From my ongoing research I have come to better understand why it is that making relationships is at the heart of the learning process for children. It is because they learn through their interactions with expert others (Vygotsky, 1978; 1986). These experts might be adults or they might be other children who are further forward within their Zone of Proximal Development (ZPD) (Vygotsky, 1978). The ZPD lies ahead of the child's current knowledge and understanding but is the place to which they have the potential to travel with the right kind of support from expert others – either children or adults. Within early years settings, I would argue, practitioners need to understand the centrality of these relationships for all young children, babies, toddlers and beyond and that the nature and needs of those relationships changes as the child grows older, more mobile and more independent and knowledgeable. In early years settings, children are right at the heart of a learning community of other children and of adults and through their play, they begin to share their knowledge and understanding of the world to sustain and develop their play themes. A central part of these processes relates to the actions and decisions of the adults around the child and although this chapter focuses on 'making relationships', those decisions or the 'pedagogies of play' are also important. I don't have time to look at these at length but Wood's work (2004; 2007; 2008 and Wood and Attfield 2005) would be useful reading.

At the heart of any successful relationship – for adults or children – is the right to make choices from a range of possibilities. The ability to make choices is a skill and has to be learned; this means it has to be practiced and a good early years environment is one where children gets lots of practice appropriate to their developing abilities and knowledge. Much of this, of course, they do through play and much of their playful learning comes through their engagements with others – hence the need for a capacity to develop good relationships.

The tasks in this chapter are based quite extensively on observation. This is because practitioners need to develop a capacity to understand how relationship building is linked with learning as children grow, play and learn in early years settings in their communities of learning. Rogoff (1997) describes development as a transformation of participation; the community within which the child spends time (whether at home or in early childhood settings) is therefore crucial to this development. However, observing learning, is by no means a simple task. As Carr (2007:109) points out, it is difficult to describe a trail of specific evidence of learning. She also talks about (2007: 111) describing learning 'with reference to the local opportunities to learn'; that is, understanding how the pedagogical decisions that adults make influence the learning opportunities that children do or do not have. Carr also places relationships at the heart of the learning process when she writes (2007:16):

> Reciprocal relationships and opportunities for participation, valuable in the here and now of an early childhood setting, are also pivotal to the first messages about the self as a learner that children receive in early childhood settings, messages that have an enduring effect on their capacities to learn in later years.

The chapter is presented in four sections:

- How children build friendships through play
- How resources, objects and artefacts help to build relationships
- How language and problem-solving builds relationships
- How conflict resolution builds relationships

How children build friendships through play

'Will you be my friend?' 'We're friends aren't we?' 'Andrew won't be friends with me.'

All practitioners hear these words at some time usually from three- and four-year-olds who are still building their own personal understanding of what it means to have a friend or to be a friend. We tend to respond with rather bland statements like: '*We are all friends here*' or '*Andrew, play nicely with Ashley, you are making him cry.*' The concept of friendship is a complex one. Just consider, when did you last make a new friend, what brought the friendship about, how did it grow and develop from an acquaintance to a friendship and why? Some friendships are forged in a moment and last a lifetime and some take a long

Photograph 3.1 Adult and child interacting (© P. Hopkins)

time to build, perhaps because of limited contacts. We might assume that because children share their early years setting with other children on a daily basis that they come to know them quickly or easily but this is not necessarily the case. It takes a long time to learn all the other children's names and it's likely that on a day-to-day basis, children have contacts with only a small number of other children. Once they can crawl, toddle and walk, they extend their range of possible contacts, they give and take toys, begin to exchange smiles and hugs and babble and watch what other children are doing. Watching other children and beginning to make eye contact and exchange smiles are key activities in making relationships for very young children. These activities should be modelled as often as possible by key workers, parents and the significant adults in their lives.

Case study

Robbie is one-month-old and visiting his grandmother with his mother and his Aunt. His Grandmother's friend is also present. The Grandmother and friend each greet him with smiles and face-to-face contact. He stares at each of them for several seconds focusing on their faces. The adults begin and maintain conversations around him. Sometimes he turns his head in the direction of voices and an adult may engage with him with a low voice, a smile and positioning their face where he can see and study it. After a while Robbie begins to get restless and agitated. Grandmother takes him and puts him over her shoulder but he remains restless. She sits him facing forward against her body. Her friend opens a magazine and places it in front of Robbie. He focuses his eyes on the pictures. She begins to turn the pages and his gaze remains attracted to images with bright colours. Pages of print are not of interest and he turns away. As she turns over one page, a large and pleasant female face is revealed. It is smiling. Robbie becomes alert and very interested. His eyes widen, his body becomes more erect, his fists open and close on extended arms. When the page is turned, he loses interest again. His mother and Aunt comment on this response and the friend turns the page back to the face. Robbie responds again in exactly the same way and continues to do so for several minutes returning his gaze to the face whenever it is presented to him. After a while he becomes agitated and loses interest altogether.

Reflection: Clearly Robbie is not making friends with the smiling face. But his deep interest shows us that he finds this engagement stimulating and rewarding and that

Case study—Cont'd

even at such an early age, he already recognizes the human face as being of great interest to him. The face is the source of his new relationships with unfamiliar others at this time – his relationship with his mother as a very familiar adult is wider-reaching than this of course. But he is already beginning to understand in his one-month-old way that the face (a pleasant, smiling face) is something worth engaging with.

Reflection for early career professional

Try showing a range of faces and other objects to babies and toddlers and see how they respond. Talk quietly and point at the pictures as you look and make eye contact yourself with the young child as often as you can – this has implication for how you sit in relation to the young child's face; voices are also important as the children begin to recognize the meanings of sound and familiar voices alongside the mental stimulation of bold, large images.

Reflection for leader/manager

Encourage staff to undertake this task and to share their reflections and findings during a staff discussion time. Has anyone been especially surprised by responses? Such incidents can be especially illuminating in deepening our understanding of the learning process.

Rubin (1980:38) notes that young children around 3 years of age may view friends as 'momentary physical playmates'; that the friendship may be based on regular but sometimes quite brief encounters. As children become older and can recall the past and project into the future (around 5 to 6 years) they begin to understand the potential permanence of friendship. In their play, I have seen older children seek out and return to favourite play themes with familiar groups of children if those resources and materials are available to them on a day to day basis – we'll look at an example of this in a later section. In my observations over the years, I have seen many examples of younger children (around 3 years of age) engaged in the ways described in the following case study. All the children here are 3-year-olds.

Case study

Four boys and two girls are chasing in a line around the outdoor play area. They are all laughing and occasionally one calls out something to the others, such as 'Catch me' or 'I'm running fast'. They stop and gather together, they laugh and make eye contact, a boy pushes a girl and she pushes him back. She frowns and then they both laugh. The boy sets off running and the others fall into a line behind him, shouting and laughing as they run. They weave around other children sometimes getting very close. Sometimes other children look alarmed as they rush past but then return to their play. The lead boy throws himself on the grass and the two other boys and one girl pile on top of him; all are laughing and shouting short phrases to one another: 'I'm on top'; 'I'm at the bottom' 'Ouch you're hurting'. The remaining girl watches them and is laughing but does not join the pile up. They stand up and the two girls go inside to the home corner where they begin to play. One boy goes inside to build with bricks and the remaining two boys go together to the climbing frame. The remaining boy watches them go but does not follow them. He goes to a bicycle and plays alone.

Reflection: These 3-year-olds are quite new to the nursery setting and are just beginning to get to know one another. They do not use one another's names as they play; their language is developing and they still speak in quite short sentences, often commenting on what they are doing as a way of thinking aloud. The line running makes few intellectual requirements of them. It's a simple and pleasurable way of interacting and they all seem to understand that smiling and laughter show that no harm is intended. Once they have had enough of this play, they move on to other activities. Some of them seem to be developing closer relationships with other children but we see that this is gendered – the girls move off together and two of the boys move off together. As Tovey (2007:24) notes, this kind of play is more than just 'playing about'. It is also important for maintaining friendships and for developing communication skills through encoding and decoding a whole range of shared signals. It involves self-restraint and turn taking – who goes 'on top' or who leads. It also she notes: 'involves close camaraderie as children enjoy the close physical contact, the thrill of the chase, the conspiratorial enjoyment of doing things that are not what they seem to be'. Let us move on to look more closely at how language and problem-solving become key elements in making relationships in the early years.

Reflection for early career professional

These children are engaging in rough and tumble play, a common form of peer interaction throughout the school years (Smith, 2005). Adults often interpret it as

Case study—Cont'd

aggressive play but children themselves come to see differences and use play faces to signal how they feel about the play (Jarvis, 2008). Try and observe children's running and play fighting activities without intervening to see how children take them forward.

- How do you think young children are using these different kinds of physical activities to build relationships with other children?
- What do they do when they finish playing in such physical ways – do they tend to move to quieter activities as these children did?
- Do you think it matters that one boy is left alone in the above play?

Reflection for leader/manager

Access some of the references from this section or similar and do some preliminary reading.

- Consider leading a discussion about rough and tumble play and about how people feel about it; how do YOU feel about it?
- Undertake some observations yourself to see how children manage rough and tumble play and whether you feel it adds anything to their learning and development. Try and listen to the play themes that underpin their play. You will often find these repeated as children become better able to share their own ideas with more familiar peers. It is important to model extended observation as a route to better understanding the learning process.

Photograph 3.2 Rough and tumble play

How resources, objects and artefacts help to build relationships

For children in early years settings, one of their earliest forms of communication might be to give and receive objects; throwing one's toys from a pram is communication. It's an invitation, based on past experience, to engage in the kind of smiling, eye contact, laughter and engagement with adult-language that we saw in the Robbie vignette above. By giving and taking objects, the young child comes to understand that a relationship can be formed. Vygotsky (1978) has also looked at the importance of objects or tools as he calls them in helping young children and indeed adults to deepen their understanding of the world. He says that tools change us (has being able to use a computer changed you? It's a tool). Saxe (1989), in building on Vygotsky's work emphasized the importance of conventions or artefacts in mediating children's learning with peers within particular contexts whereby prior understandings are shared through cooperation. The children in the above case study had prior understandings about running and chasing (not involving objects) that allowed them to cooperate.

Objects have a purpose and we have to learn that purpose (problem-solving). When a child first encounters bricks, they may throw them because 'ball' might be well-embedded in their understanding of the world and a brick may remind them of a ball, especially if they have had a recent and happy experience with a ball. If the adult models building with the bricks in a tower, the child will usually imitate this if the new idea has meaning for them. The child may build for a while and then throw the brick again, remembering this more familiar action. It may be better to replace the brick with soft balls at this point, rather than to insist to a young child that 'throwing bricks is dangerous and must stop'. Although the child may move away from the bricks, my own observations have shown as has the work of others that once a child has encountered a new idea, they will often return to it at another point, especially if a sensitive key adult understands that building may be a new concept and that it could be appropriate to return the child to the activity the next day – if they are interested. We cannot force interest anymore than we force language.

In the next case study we will see the beginnings of shared understandings around objects and in section three we will see some children interacting around objects in complex and demanding ways; children I would argue, who have had time to build their shared understandings from prior experience together and who can now take advantage of the local opportunities that Carr (2007) talked about above.

Case study

Sofia is just 3 years old and new to the early years setting. She stays close to her key worker as she plays in the home corner, opening and closing doors, putting objects on the floor, hugging a doll and lying on the bed. She goes across to the sand tray with the doll and a teacup and looks into it; she looks to see if her key worker is close and she is, although talking to another child. Sofia sees buckets and spades but appears to ignore them. She takes the teacup and fills it with sand and offers the 'drink' to her doll. Another child, older and with more experience in the setting, comes over and watches. She goes to the home corner and gets another doll, a teacup and some pots and pans and brings them to the sand tray. She takes out the buckets and spades and places them on the floor and sits her doll in the sand tray and places the 'pots and pans' around then. Sofia smiles and copies this, sitting her own doll in the tray. They exchange smiles and the older gild starts to talk about what she is doing. Sofia has English as a second language but she smiles and copies some of the actions. A third child goes over to the key worker and says: 'They have got dolls in the sand and things from the home corner'. It seems the key worker is expected to act but what should she do?

Reflection for early years professional

- Discuss the above case study together with other staff. What you think should happen next?
- How comfortable do you feel with children using objects for purposes that are different from the ones for which adults think they are intended?
- What will be the implications of any decisions you make for how Sofia or the child with whom she is beginning to play might use resources or play together in the future?

Reflection for leader/ manager

- Discuss this case study at a staff meeting. Explore the outcomes of all the possible responses that an adult might make at this point. Does this reflect your decision about what the adult should do?
- What other examples have you and other staff seen of children transporting objects around their setting and for what reasons do you think they do it?
- What are the implications of any decisions you make for children's play and the way resources are used in the future?

How language and problem-solving builds relationships

We know that language is at the heart of the learning process. It is not the only way in which children (or adults) make meaning in the world however; they do this also through drawing for example (Anning and Ring, 2004; Pahl, 2002) through mark making (Carruthers and Worthington, 2006; Worthington, 2010) and through their symbolic representations in play. Some children make meaning through the use of computers and the internet at quite an early age, depending on their home circumstances (Yelland et al.; 2008; Marsh, 2004; 2005). Children have many modes for learning how to communicate and we now talk about 'multi-modality': 'a concept of communication that subsumes the written, the visual, the gestural and the tactile' (Pahl and Roswell 2005:26). However, spoken language is powerful because it can allow us to convey quite complicated ideas quite quickly – once we have mastered it. Language is the brain in full flight towards new kinds of understanding and towards learning. We can learn when we are alone once we have mastered new ways to access information but for young children speaking and listening is an important way of coming to understand the world. Egan (1988) was long ago critical of the way in which formal schooling, where adults over-direct children's learning experiences, can rob the child of their oral cultures within which their own identity and sense of self is rooted. Our schools have, for a long time, prioritized literacy over language and ignored the richness of the young child's 'multi-modality' (Yelland et al.; 2008|). By focusing on language in this section as integral to relationship building I am not therefore wanting to convey the sense that other forms of communication are not important and should not be nurtured through early years provision but what I want to do in this section is to share some insights into the ways in which language can be stimulated and developed through play. I also want to link language use to problem-solving as a key activity for all young children. Because of this, it also becomes a key responsibility for adults to create and sustain opportunities where children quite naturally use language to solve problems through their playful encounters with peers and adults.

When a brick becomes a telephone or a mobile phone, a child is making meaning. The child is also simultaneously solving a problem; they need to 'talk' to someone at a distance; they need a machine to do this. They have learned to understand that communication can be facilitated by machines (even though the young child might not think of it in exactly this way). They are not just imitating what they have seen; they are simultaneously, in their own way, thinking about what this means. The child is thinking, doing and using language simultaneously and may be as young as 2 1/2 years – quite an achievement. Language exists to allow us to communicate; those of us who are fluent take it for granted – until we try to learn a foreign language and then we return to some degree of understanding of what a young child must learn to do in order to learn language to communicate. Like all skills it needs practice and as Brock (1999: xiii) says at the start of her edited book: 'Language, whether first, second or subsequent, is learned in context'. If we go back again to the vignette with Robbie, we can begin to see how he might be beginning to connect sound with faces; the sight of a face might be associated with sounds and hence the original excitement at the magazine face. But it can present no further stimulation so interest is lost. However, his mother, his Aunt and his grannie all make interesting noises too; this is an integral part of his relationship with them and the very early beginnings of understanding about communication. Language is about sharing meaning, gaining new information, interesting facts, ideas and possibilities.

So young children make meaning through their play with peers by combining language with action and inter-action as shall be illustrated in the next vignette. Like Robbie and the adults who love him, they do not necessarily need to be at the same level of language development in order to make meaning together. When children play in groups (as we saw with the line running above) those with well-developed language can model it for others and are likely to be much closer to other children's levels of competence with language than adults will be. In this way, the children can become the 'expert others' that Vygotsky speaks of (1978). This next extract from my research shows an extensive period of problem-solving. These children are 4- and 5-year-olds in a reception classroom. This vignette was first shared in Broadhead (2004) but I want to present it a little differently here to tease out the specific links between language, action, inter-action and problem-solving as children play with open-ended play materials or 'the whatever you want it to be place' as is briefly explained before moving on to the vignette.

Within my own research across the 3–6 age range, in nursery, reception and year 1 settings, the richest use of children's language in play and the highest levels of cooperation I have seen have been in the 'whatever you want it to be place' (Broadhead, 2004; 2010). This grew out of joint research with reception teachers when we discovered that role play in the home corner, a cafe or a shop, produced very little cooperative play while sand and construction play produced high levels of cooperation and quite complex problem-solving scenarios in children's play. The next case study, as well as showing complex uses of objects while children interact, is also an example of the 'whatever you want it to be place'. In such a space, the resources or materials aim to be as open-ended as possible. They don't of themselves, suggest particular themes to the children (in the way a stethoscope suggests hospitals) but allow the themes that emerge from the children's minds to be explored. The case study below is based around a wooden clothes horse that is flexible enough to use in different arrangements; in my work with educators they have often used cardboard boxes, large pieces of fabric and other open-ended materials to create the same levels of opportunity for children to come together in sharing their ideas and in using the materials in different ways to explore the themes that come to mind as they play.

Photograph 3.3 Children playing with cardboard boxes (photograph by L. Nahmad-Williams)

Case study

On the carpet, the children have an old wooden clothes horse, pieces of fabric and pegs and cushions. During play, they also transfer buckets and plastic chairs into the

Case study—Cont'd

area as their ideas developed. Three girls and a boy were playing together although at first; one of the girls developed a party theme and watched the others as they worked together. The three work together to design a house, draping fabric over the clothes horse. It keeps falling off and they have to try different ways of attaching it (*problem-solving*). When finished they seem dissatisfied and one girl says: 'I think our house is too small' (*a mathematical judgement and relevant as there are four of them; it looks small for four people*). They look at it and the boy announces: 'well let's make a tent' and begins to re-direct them. He then says: 'let's make a cave' as if he has imagined a tent and feels it will still be too small but that caves are big. (*I don't know if he's ever seen a cave or a tent but I guess he may have at least have seen pictures and has already some sense of scale to draw on; you do get the sense that he is drawing on prior knowledge and bringing it to the fore in solving the problem of sufficient space.*) One girl replies: 'I'll get a table' but the boy replies: 'You don't have tables in a cave'. (*This is imaginative play but perhaps the context needs to feel real to the boy to match an image in his head.*) But she persists: 'We'll need one for the party', drawing perhaps on the comments from the 'separate' girl who is making a party. The table arrives as a bucket and is accepted. (*Negotiation successful; problem solved.*) The boy then suggests they make a roller coaster and they turn the clothes horse over and use buckets and chairs to sit 'inside' holding onto the side and rocking it. They use language to develop imaginary themes with which they all connect quite quickly: 'Get in dad' to the boy and 'we're in a tunnel'. The boy wants to bring a large cushion into the roller coaster; the girls push it out playfully as if teasing him and he pushes it back, smiling – a pleasant 'contest of wills' which the boy either wins or is allowed to win, depending on your interpretation. The girls cease to resist (*problem solved*). The play becomes boisterous and gradually the structure tumbles and the children with it. They laugh but are not hurt and the boy re-designs it saying: 'I'll make it comfier for you' (*showing caring and friendship*). The play becomes very boisterous and results in a heap of children under the tumbled construction. They stand and look concerned as two appear slightly hurt. But this passes without any adult intervention (both the class teacher and I have observed this play for almost an hour) and one girl says: EEh I'm hot, let's take our cardies off, enough roller coaster for one day I think. The boy remarks: 'Let's make a cave' and quieter play begins as the children self-regulate their play.

Reflection: Objects are most transformative when they are sufficiently open and flexible in connecting with the ideas, interests and experiences that come to mind for children as they play (Nutbrown, 1994). Drawing from my own research I have illustrated many times how the 'whatever you want it to be place' brings children together by providing an open-ended forum in which their own interests, themes, pre-occupations and ideas can inter-connect. I do not know that all four children had ever seen a roller coaster but they could understand from watching and listening to the boy what they needed to do and the resulting play showed potentially deep levels of friendship and good relationships across these older children who have had chances to play together and become very familiar with one another. Their oral culture was strong and was shared and meaning was made through language and through imaginative use of objects and spaces.

Practical task

- Try and identify some children, of any age, who play together on a regular basis. Try and observe them on a regular basis over a period of about 1 month. You may have to look for opportunities based on when you see them together; this may not be something that you can plan to do at a specific time and place. Do not place the children together but seek to observe them when they have chosen to be together. Try to listen to their play to see what play themes they are engaging with. Identify the problems they encounter either imaginative or real (as in the vignette above) and how they work together to solve the problem and in particular how they use language or other forms of communication to solve their problems. Try and observe them over a long period as we did above (almost an hour) because you may see a time lapse between problems set and problem solved. You might also see how their play themes ebb and flow; how they are often re-captured after a time lapse and re-invigorated with new possibilities. As you begin to build this store of information and knowledge start to think about what you could do to improve the learning environment for these children. Could you provide them with more materials or allow them to use the materials in a different way? Might there be stories you could read to them or other activities that you could engage in with them to help to develop their understanding of the themes and ideas they are choosing to engage with. Supporting language development through play does not always have to mean playing with the children. You can give them ideas and experiences that can feed into their play at a later date and develop their vocabulary and their understanding of how the world works. In this way, you are tuning into the children's shared interests.

Case study—Cont'd

Reflection for early career professional

- First of all, think back to what Carr talked about earlier in the chapter in relation to 'local opportunities'. What have the adults in this classroom done to create this challenging problem-solving and language rich environment for these interacting players?
- How could you use your extended observations to inform your future practice?

Reflection for leader/manager

- Your staff may be more familiar with relatively brief observations that focus on individual children in order to assess specific learning outcomes. The above task is suggesting a very different kind of format and approach to observation, something that this chapter overall is seeking to promote. It asks staff to gather information over a period of time in order to bring deep, personal meanings to what the children are trying to achieve in their play including how they use language to help them achieve their goals. Staff may feel that they need 'permission' to use their time in this way and it may also be helpful for staff to talk together about their intentions to observe and how other colleagues might support this in different ways.

How conflict resolution builds relationships

Adults can often become concerned when children experience conflict and engage in conflicting ways with peers. But it may be that even quite young children can resolve conflicts for themselves if the adults around them can create opportunities for children to acquire these skills. In my own observations, I have always said to practitioners that I would not become involved in children's play unless I felt children were at risk of harm. As a result, I have let several periods of conflict become resolved by the children and then seen how their play has become more complex and interactive as a result of the conflict resolution (Broadhead, 2010). Very often the conflict is short-lived and very seldom have I seen acts of violence by young children. I have seen some hefty pushes and pulls but I have seen resolution of this by the children themselves. Young children's social conflicts are often about object sharing and Hay and Ross (1982) showed them engaging in object disputes in which children use toys as bargaining tools for social interaction. This is quite common in my experience. We looked in section two at the importance of objects for children; if they are tools that shape knowledge then it's no wonder children want to keep hold of them or gain access to them.

While I was observing play in an early years unit recently, I watched two boys playing. Their play centred upon a large plastic drum that they had filled with bricks. One boy, Sam, was 'shovelling' the bricks out of the drum into a pile (it was a fire). He had a good-sized spade and was deeply engaged in the task. The other boy (Jan who has English as a second language) was putting bricks into the fire and they were developing the play theme together. Sam placed his spade on the floor and went to get some water. Jan picked the spade up and began to use it. Sam returned, dropped his water and went to grab the spade. A tussle ensued with each child pulling at the spade. Jan looked at me and his look seemed to say: 'Please sort this out'. I could not ignore it. As I went to them I noticed a similar spade on the floor just inside the unit. I pointed this out to Jan who immediately ran indoors and came out with his spade, very happy. Together the boys developed the play for an extended period. Neither boy had much language but they spent over half an hour in combined play, sharing ideas and developing the theme around the plastic drum and its contents. In order to fully engage in the play, as he 'saw' it, Jan needed a spade. It was central to the play theme and to a deep level of engagement with the theme and with the roles they were each taking. It was not enough to 'share'; sharing would have diminished their minute by minute involvement. The remainder of their play was close and cooperative. Had I delivered a lecture on sharing, I suspect the child without the spade might have walked away and missed what I think turned into an important opportunity for these two boys, both relatively new to the setting, to learn that they had common interests. A few minutes later, Jan put his spade down and another boy came to take it. With an alarmed look on his face, Jan went to seize it back and another tussle began. A student teacher came across and asked me who had it first. I explained to the third boy that Jan was playing with it but had put it down while he went to fetch some water and that I didn't think he had finished with it. The 4-year-old seemed satisfied with this answer and left the play. Jan and Sam continued.

Butovskaya et al. (2000) reviewed four international studies showing that young children can make peace after conflict, and increasingly so as they become older, if opportunities present themselves in their daily lives to practise and develop the associated skills of conflict resolution. Their review revealed cultural influences on the inclination to make peace after conflict and it appears at an earlier age in cultures where cooperation and kinship are highly valued as cultural norms. As my own research has progressed over the years, I have often considered whether our early years settings really do encourage the kinds of cooperation where children build and extend their repertoires of conflict resolution rather than relying on adults to settle disputes with their own decisions. I understood the importance of the spade to Jan and Sam because I was watching the play over a period of time. I can recall times as a teacher when I have said: 'well you've had it for a long time, it's time for someone else to have a go'; without ever realizing that I could not only be potentially stopping a very important play experience but might also be inadvertently separating inter-acting peers who are building their repertoires of social interaction in very meaningful ways through their play.

Early career professional

I am not by any means suggesting that you allow children to come to physical harm, but next time you see conflict, think about holding back for a few minutes to see what children do and how they subsequently respond to one another if they are able to resolve the conflict themselves. Share your findings in discussion with colleagues. In addition, talk together about what you feel you do, as practitioners, to help children to develop their skills of conflict resolution and to become cooperative and by 'cooperative' I don't just mean 'playing together' but also 'setting and solving problems together as they play'.

Leader/Manager

Be sensitive to the fact that staff may deliberately not be intervening in what may appear to you to be an instance of conflict between children. Join in the discussions and support staff in being able to talk openly about what they felt and how the instance developed. It can make staff feel uneasy to be seemingly seen to be condoning conflict but children are often more skilful than we think at bringing about a resolution. Talk with staff also about what you think you do in the setting to help children be cooperative and to set and solve problems together. Where are the places where this happens and how might they be further developed?

Conclusion

The four sections of this chapter have aimed to bring 'making relationships' 'alive' as being inherently linked to children's opportunities for learning in early years settings. We are talking about many forms of learning here including intellectual, emotional, social and moral. As we have known for a long time, play is at the heart of learning for young children and yet it remains difficult to specifically link play with learning for individual or groups of children (Moyles, 2005; Pramling Samuelsson and Asplund Carlsson, 2008). I have argued here and elsewhere (Broadhead, 2006) as have others, that observing children's play is the key to understanding the learning process. It is also the key to understanding how we can become more effective practitioners and provide pedagogies of learning through play in the early years settings in which we work. Most importantly for this chapter, by observing children we can come to better understand how their friendships and relationships are integral to these learning processes and how we can support the growth of relationships and friendships from the very early years onwards if we know and understand their significance for children.

References

Anning, A. and Ring, K. (2004) *Making Sense of Children's Drawings*. Maidenhead: Open University Press

Broadhead, P. (2001) 'Investigating sociability and cooperation in four and five year olds in reception class settings'. *International Journal of Early Years Education,* 9 (1) 23–35

Broadhead, P. (2004) *Early Years Play and Learning: Developing Social Skills and Cooperation*. London: RoutledgeFalmer

Broadhead, P. (2006) 'Developing an understanding of young children's learning through play: the place of observation, interaction and reflection'. *British Educational Research Journal*, 32 (2) 191–207

Broadhead, P. (2010) 'Cooperative play and learning from nursery to year one', in P. Broadhead, J. Howard and E. Wood (eds) *Play and Learning in the Early Years*. London: Sage Publications

Broadhead, P. (2010) 'Conflict resolution and children's behaviour: Observing and understanding social and cooperative play in early years educational settings'. *Early Years: An International Journal of Research and Development*

Brock, A. (1999) (ed.) *Into the Enchanted Forest*. Stoke on Trent: Trentham Books

Butovskaya, M., Verbeek, P., Ljungberg, T. and Lunardini, A. (2000) 'A multicultural view of peacemaking among young children', in F. Aureli, and F. B. M. de Waal (eds) *Natural Conflict Resolution*. Berkeley and Los Angeles: University of California Press

Carr, M. (2007) *Assessment in Early Childhood Settings: Learning Stories*. London: Sage Publications

Carruthers, E. and Worthington, M. (2006) *Children's Mathematics, Making Marks, Making Meaning*. London: Sage Publications (2nd edition)

Egan, K. (1988) *Primary Understanding, Education in Early Childhood*. London: Routledge

Hay, D. F. and Ross, H. S. (1982) 'The social nature of early conflict'. *Child Development,* 53, 105–113

Jarvis, P. (2008) 'The usefulness of play', in A. Brock, S. Dodds, P. Jarvis and Y. Olusoga (eds) *Perspectives on Play*. Pearson: Harlow, pp. 11–19

Marsh, J. (2004) *BBC Child of Our Time: Young Children's Use of Popular Culture, Media and New Technologies*. Sheffield: University of Sheffield

Marsh, J. (2005) *Popular Culture, New Media and Digital Literacy in Early Childhood Education*. London: RoutledgeFalmer

Moyles, J. (2005) (ed.) *The Excellence of Play*. Maidenhead: Open University Press (2nd edition)

Nutbrown, C. (1994) *Threads of Thinking*. London: Paul Chapman Publishing

Pahl, K. (2002) 'Ephemera, mess and miscellaneous piles; texts and practices in families'. *Journal of Early Childhood Literacy,* 2(2) 145–166

Pahl, K. and Roswell, J. (2005) *Literacy and Education: Understanding the New Literacy Studies in the Classroom*. London: Paul Chapman

Pramling Samuelsson, I. and Asplund Carlsson, M. (2008) 'The playing learning child: Towards a pedagogy of early childhood'. *Scandinavian Journal of Educational Research,* 52 (6) 623–641

Rogoff, B. (1997) 'Evaluating development in the process of participation: Theory methods and practice building on each other', in E. Amsel and K. Ann Renninger (eds) *Change and Development: Issues of Theory, Method and Evaluation*. Mahwah, NJ and London: Erlbaum

Rubin, Z. (1980) *Children's Friendships*. Fontana paperbacks, Glasgow

Saxe, G. B. (1989) 'Transfer of learning across cultural practices', *Cognition and Instruction,* 6 (4) 325–330

Smith, P. (2005) 'Physical activity and rough and tumble play', in J. Moyles (ed.) *The Excellence of Play* (2nd edition). Maidenhead: Open University Press

Tovey, H. (2007) *Playing Outdoors*. Maidenhead: Open University Press

Vygotsky, L. S. (1978) *Mind in Society: The Development of Higher Psychological Processes*. London: Harvard University Press

Vygotsky, L. S. (1986) *Thought and Language,* translation revised and edited by A. Kozulin, Cambridge MA: MIT Press

Wood, E. (2004) 'Developing a pedagogy of play', in A. Anning, J. Cullen and M. Fleer (eds) *Early Childhood Education*. London: Sage Publications

Wood, E. (2007) 'New directions in play: Consensus or collision'. *Education, 3–13.* 35(4) 309–320

Wood, E. (2008) 'Everyday play activities as therapeutic and pedagogical encounters'. *European Journal of Psychotherapy & Counselling,* 10(2) 111–120

Wood, E. and Attfield, J. (2005) *Play, Learning and the Early Childhood Curriculum* (2nd edition). London: Paul Chapman Publishing

Worthington, M. (2010) 'Play as a complex landscape: Imagination and symbolic meanings', in P. Broadhead, J. Howard and E. Wood (eds) *Play and Learning in the Early Years*. London: Sage Publications

Yelland, N., Lee, L., O'Rourke, M. and Harrison, C. (2008) *Re-thinking Learning in Early Childhood Education*. Maidenhead: Open University Press

Behaviour and Self-Control 4

Introduction

Children are all unique and come from many different families and backgrounds. They develop cognitively, linguistically, physically, socially and emotionally at different rates and in different ways. They all have individual experiences which shape their development and behaviour. Most children will have had loving and secure experiences where their families have loved and cared for them and meet their needs well. These children are more likely to be able to employ the types of behaviours needed to engage in learning and make and maintain successful relationships. Some children may not have had such positive experiences; need more support to feel valued, safe and secure if they are going to be competent learners, resilient, capable, confident and self-assured and demonstrate and meet behaviour expectations. This is one of the key principles underpinning the Early Years Foundation Stage (DCSF, 2008a). Practitioners need to be able to support the needs of all children and help them develop the self-confidence and self-esteem and prosocial behaviours they will need to become happy, healthy adults and effective learners. They will be able to do this if they have a good grasp of how children develop: by getting to know the children they care for and maintaining caring and trusting relationships and providing the structure and guidance children need in a warm and secure environment.

There is some debate about whether children's behaviour is deteriorating and whether or not children behave as well now as they may have in the past. This has been a debate in many new generations and it is hard to measure because as society changes so do expectations of behaviour and what one person views as rude another may view as assertive. The press can sometimes give the impression that all children are out of control which is patently not the case. However families may face great demands in terms of family break-down, separation, financial issues and isolation which will impact on children and their feelings of safety and security. It is true that the future will demand citizens who have effective learning skills and excellent social skills and have the flexibility and adaptability to deal with rapid change. Practitioners and education settings are a very important part of helping children acquire the necessary skills and self-confidence they will need for the future.

All children display inappropriate behaviour sometimes; this may include children being silly by teasing or detracting others; this can lead to children disrupting their own or others' learning. Sometimes children may be defiant when they refuse to follow adult direction and sometimes aggressive where children are violent physically or verbally towards others. There are degrees of severity and this can range from mild teasing or irritating others to more serious acts of violence such as kicking and biting. Children can behave in these ways for a variety of reasons: they may be frustrated, be unable to communicate their needs, tired or just don't know what the acceptable behaviour might be in that context (Papatheodorou, 2005). Sometimes children's level of development and maturity means that they are unable to behave in a way the practitioner expects. The behaviour is then interpreted by practitioners and unless they have the knowledge and expertise of how children develop they may misinterpret the behaviour and sometimes this can lead to children being labelled as 'naughty' or a 'problem child' (Upton, 1992). This is not helpful to the child and can lead children to see themselves in a negative light which will inevitably affect their confidence and self-esteem. It is important that practitioners working with children discuss the different ways children may behave and come to some consensus about what is acceptable behaviour as sometimes different people have different thresholds of what they may consider is naughty or unacceptable behaviour.

Understanding development in relation to behaviour and self-control

Understanding how children develop emotionally, socially, cognitively, physically and morally can help practitioners support children in developing appropriate and acceptable behaviour and self-control. Feelings and emotions underpin most behaviour and therefore practitioners need to support children emotionally and help them understand their emotions and how they may affect their behaviour (Goleman, 1996). For children to be able to form relationships and become aware of the needs of others they need to know how to behave socially, so practitioners need to understand how children may develop socially and how they can support them. For children to be able to make sense of their emotions and develop socially they need thought and language and ability to reason. In order for children to be able to make choices about how to behave they need to understand what is acceptable behaviour in the culture they live in and be able to make judgements about what is right and wrong. Children will develop at different rates but a broad understanding of how they develop will help practitioners support and manage behaviour.

Behaviour and self-control from birth to 3 years of age

Children under the age of 12 months need to feel safe and secure with the adults they come into contact with. Therefore it is important that the adults spend time with the child and become familiar with the child's needs and moods. They will eventually be able to recognize when a child needs feeding or sleep, or if they need to be soothed or reassured. They will communicate with the child by touch and facial expressions and talk. They will become attuned to the needs of the child and by meeting these needs they will be able to care and support for the child within a routine that is flexible enough to do so and in which the child feels safe and secure. If the practitioner understands the importance of getting to know and respond to babies in their care and then builds a close and trusting relationship with them and their parents this will provide a good foundation for children to start to understand their own behaviour and develop self-control (DCSF, 2008b).

As children start to grow and become more mobile and start to talk they become more aware of others. However they are still unsure of what they can do and their physical skills are still developing. So a child may drop things or spill things or bump into things. At this stage the practitioner needs to be aware of the environment and provide safety and security but still allow children freedom to explore and develop. Sometimes practitioners can become frustrated or annoyed with children who drop things or bump into others and interpret it as unacceptable behaviour when in fact it is to do with physical immaturity. This can be particularly true when children are able to run but find it difficult to navigate or stop. The practitioner must think carefully about the environment and how it can be adapted to the needs of the child in order to help the child to interact in the best way.

As children start to develop language they may be able to start expressing simple needs such as wanting a biscuit. However it takes time for children to be able to fully communicate their needs (Rodd, 1996) and they may continue to cry and throw tantrums if they feel their needs are not being met. Again, this can be interpreted as unacceptable behaviour rather than the frustration it is, so it is still important that adults take time to get to know the child and to be able to respond to their needs as sensitively as possible. Even though children may be starting to develop more complex sentences by the age of 3, they may not be able to respond to adults talking to them about their behaviour, as they are not always able to comprehend meaning.

Emotionally they need the security of a familiar adult and comfort when things go wrong. The reassurance of a familiar adult in sight can act as a calming influence for many children. Children of 2 to 3 years old are starting to recognize themselves as individuals and start to assert their independence and try to control (Erickson, 1963). For example if you ask them to put on their coat they may refuse. Again this may be interpreted as unacceptable behaviour and a battle of wills may follow but if a choice is offered for example, 'Do you want to put on your coat or wellies first?' it allows for some choice and control. A practitioner needs to recognize the developing needs of children at this age; sometimes they need to be close and reassured but they also may want to explore their independence and opportunities to take control should be provided. This will depend on each child's maturity but will also change depending on the context or the mood of the child.

Photograph 4.1 Child showing frustration (© P. Hopkins)

Socially children are starting to be much more aware of others and gravitate towards other children. However, they have not learned many of the social skills they need to always mange this successfully so they may snatch toys if they want them. They find it difficult to wait or take turns at this stage without adult support (Lindon, 1997). They may become frustrated and hit people or throw things. Practitioners in this situation needs to put boundaries in place by clearly saying 'no hitting' or ' no throwing' but they also need to start helping children understand that such actions can hurt. Simple stories can be a good way to do this. For example using a persona doll to tell the story of what happened when someone threw some lego and it hit the doll and how it made it feel. The practitioner can discuss with the character what the more appropriate behaviour would be and encourage the children to join in the discussion. They can also play with children to model appropriate behaviour and support turn taking (Pre-school Learning Alliance, 2007). For example in role play the practitioner may model appropriate ways of using please and thank you. By doing this they are starting to help children to acquire the social skills they need in a safe way. Sometimes practitioners may recognize a situation before it develops and distract or divert the child to play with something else; in this way they may help children avoid a situation which could result in conflict or distress and as a result avoiding an incident of inappropriate behaviour.

Case study

Emily is 2 years and 5 months old and started in her preschool setting 5 months ago. She settled well and had a good relationship with her key worker and other practitioners. She was familiar with routines and played happily with a group of older children; she sometimes mixed with outside of the setting. Her mother said she really enjoyed her time in the preschool and couldn't wait to get there every morning. Emily went on holiday and did not return until after the summer break in September (an 8-week break). While she was away many of the staff changed and a new manager started. The layout of the setting was changed and many of the routines were altered. As is normal, several of the older children with whom she played moved on to nursery. When Emily returned to school she gradually became more and more clingy to her mother and tearful in the morning. She started to play by herself and became quite withdrawn. She found it difficult to share with other children and refused to follow instructions. Her mother said she was starting to be sick in the mornings and practitioners noticed she seemed unhappy in the setting.

Reflection for entry career professional

- Can you identify the factors which helped Emily feel secure?
- What do you think Emily may have been feeling?
- What steps would you take to help Emily settle into the setting again?

Reflection for leader/manager

- Do you consider how changes can affect children and how you will support children manage the changes?
- How do you support children settle into the setting?
- In what ways do you enable staff and children to build secure and trusting relationships?

Behaviour and self-control from 3 to 5 years of age

As children start to become more physically adept and are able to run and climb they often seem to have a lot of energy and need opportunities to move around and a range of physical challenges. It is important for practitioners to recognize this and provide opportunities for children to be able to do this. Often children who are full of energy and run around a lot and engage in boisterous play (often, though not always, boys) (Papatheodorou, 2005) can be seen as overactive and a danger to others. Practitioners may try to stop this and where children continue to engage in this behaviour they can be labelled difficult. However practitioners need to consider the physical needs of children and provide activities and space which allow children to use this energy in a positive way but also help them to understand how running in confined spaces or hurting others is not acceptable and children get hurt.

While children do have lots of energy at this age they also can become tired, hungry and thirsty quite quickly which will have an effect on how they manage their behaviour (Lindon, 1997). Often children are unable to recognize their physical needs and associated feelings in this way so it's important for practitioners to be sensitive to children's needs and so should explore and provide for these rather than interpret a child's behaviour as a problem.

Between 3 and 5 children's language develops rapidly but at different rates for different children and it may well be that they do not always understand or are able to interpret what practitioners are saying to them. So telling children what to do does not always lead to them doing what you may have intended and this may be interpreted as a child misbehaving. So it is important that practitioners think about the language they use and check how the child has understood, or model what they want the child to do. Communication with children at this stage is not just about using language; actions can be very useful as well. This is also true of rules and routines. Children need help in understanding them and applying them, modelling them, practising them, using songs and props helps children know what they need to do and how to follow them. The practitioner could try modelling good listening by asking the children to be quiet then look and listen, this can be in conjunction with using gestures to point to the mouth, then the eyes and then the ears. This can be reinforced by using a card with a picture of the lips, eyes and ears which the practitioner can point to and use as a reminder.

As children approach 5, they are starting to be able to engage with both adults and peers and can express their needs through language and listen to a response so practitioners can start to encourage children to resolve any issues and conflicts using language but will need to ensure that children have the necessary vocabulary and support them in this process. Vygotsky is a social constructivist theorist and believed that children develop and learn in a social context and it is the interaction between the child and the person who has the skills and understanding of what they need to do (in this case the practitioner) which guides them in their learning. This joint approach to helping children think about their behaviour and solve problems enables children to gain a better understanding of their own behaviour and also how to deal with others and resolve conflicts (Vygotsky, 1962).

The Highscope approach which originated in the USA recognizes conflict as inevitable and sees conflict resolution as a learning opportunity teaching children skills of communication and negotiation. They use a problem-solving approach which involves 6 stages. First the adult must calmly stop any use of aggression, then they acknowledge the children's feelings, they then take steps to find out from all involved what the problem is and will restate the problem, next the practitioner will ask the children to offer solutions to the problem which are discussed and may be adopted or rejected by the children, in this way they have some control and see themselves in the role of problem solvers. If the children are unable to come to a solution the practitioner will offer possible solutions for the children to select. Finally the practitioner will support the children in implementing the solution and praising them for resolving the problem (Holt, 2007).

Practitioners will need to consider when they do this with children, as children will need to be calm as it will be very difficult for them if they are angry or upset. So practitioners may spend some time individually with children helping them to calm down and sort out what has happened before they bring children together.

Emotionally children are starting to be aware of themselves and their feelings. Positive feelings and a good self-concept are very important in determining appropriate behaviour. They need to have trusting relationships with practitioners who help them to feel good about themselves. They need to feel valued and that they belong and they need assistance to be successful and to receive support, encouragement and praise in response to their actions. They need their feelings to be recognized and acknowledged. If children feel that practitioners approval depends on them always being good they may start to feel insecure, anxious and even guilty. They may not be able to separate the response of the adult to their behaviour and interpret it as being about them; they may then start to see themselves as naughty or worthless. It is very important for practitioners not to emotionally distance themselves from a child as a response to them if they do behave inappropriately (DCSF, 2008a). Behaviour is a result of interactions in the setting; constant negative interactions may lead to poor behaviour.

Bowlby was theorist who believed that children needed to develop secure attachments to their mothers and if they failed to create this attachment or were deprived of it in some way it would have a detrimental effect on their future emotion development. Where children have formed secure loving attachments they are more likely to develop a positive self-identity and self-esteem (Bowlby, 1969).

The theorist Maslow suggested people have a hierarchy of needs in order to reach the most desirable emotional state and understanding which he described as Self-actualization. Once the most basic needs such as food, warmth and shelter have been met then children need to feel safe and secure. If they are then able to receive and give love and affection this will lead to positive self-esteem. If all above are in place they could finally reach Self-actualization as adults which will ensure they have a strong and positive sense of self and of the needs of others and be able to embrace life with motivation and enthusiasm. He believed if children were deprived of some of the basic needs or felt vulnerable or unloved they would find it difficult to develop a positive self-identity and self-confidence (Maslow, 1968).

While practitioners may not always be able to compensate for deficits in a child's past relationships and circumstances they can still provide strong and supportive attachments with children to make them feel secure and valued while they are in their care. This in turn can help children build a more positive self-identity and develop self-confidence. Positive and supportive interactions will help children feel good about themselves and give them the support they need to mange and control their emotions.

Socially children are starting to develop a much greater interest in peers and begin to explore friendships. They are able to demonstrate different social behaviours and increasingly able to talk to peers, cooperate with them and share. They may start to recognize how their behaviour may affect others and they will start to understand how other people's behaviour affects them. However this will depend on the experiences they have had and some children will still find it difficult. For example, an only child has not had the opportunity to develop such skills and may need more support. This can still be a challenge for children of this age and they are likely to find it difficult to negotiate all issues and may therefore feel frustrated or unhappy which can result in inappropriate and even aggressive behaviour. Practitioners need to take time to help children develop the social skills they need and provide activities which support cooperation and sharing. Routines can be useful, for example helping to prepare snacks to share with all the children can help children recognize the need for sharing and equality. Games which allow for turn taking can help children understand about waiting for their turn. They need to help children see how behaviour affects others in positive and negative ways and model good behaviour for children to observe.

For children to be able to manage their own behaviour they need to develop a moral understanding and what is right and wrong. This is linked to their social, emotional and cognitive development and practitioners need to understand it in this context.

Cognitive theorist Piaget suggests there is a staged approach to moral development. He did not believe children under 3 years old were capable of moral understanding. He suggests children of 3 to 5 years old fall into stage 1 which he called Moral Realism. In this stage he believes children have a rigid and inflexible understanding of what is right and wrong. They accept rules are made by authority figures (adults) and that they should never be broken under any circumstances; right is right and wrong is wrong. Consequences should always be severe to punish offender. Piaget called his next stage of moral development Moral Relativism, he applies to children of 5 to 9 years of age. He suggests that they are able through thought and reason to start distinguishing between intent and accident in a misdeed. They recognize that consequences should be different depending on the severity of the crime or the intent of the individual.

They are able to feel remorse for what they have done. They are also able to contribute to rules and understand the reasons for them (Piaget, 1965).

Kohlberg built on Piaget's theories and he too believed in a staged approach to developing morality. He suggests children under the age of 4 years old would not have the cognitive ability needed for moral understanding. In his first stage called Pre-conventional Morality which would apply to children 4 to 5 years old he believed that children are concerned with what happens as a result of their behaviour so the outcome, either reward or punishment will motivate their behaviour, they would only consider themselves and have little concern for others. As children start to develop through this stage they will start to have some concern and awareness of people who are close to them (Kohlberg, 1996).

Children need to learn to use appropriate behaviour in different situations, they also need to feel either intrinsically pleased or understand they are doing something wrong in relation to what they do in a situation. Finally, they need to be able to make judgements and be able to understand and choose to apply rules. This is a complex process and takes time to develop. Practitioners can help children develop a moral code and be able to apply this to their behaviour. Initially this may be through helping children understand that there are certain ways to behave in the setting. This may conflict in some instances with the home and this may confuse some children. They will need support in understanding the expectations of the setting but they can recognize this as they become more aware of their surroundings and their place within it at around 3 years old, for example a no hitting rule. But they will still find ideas of fairness difficult and may only see it in relation to themselves. So for example if a child is asked to give the bike to another child as their turn is over he may say it's not fair and display frustration or even aggression, as he only understand the world in relation to his own feelings. They have little understanding of telling lies and may take things that are not theirs because they want them. Practitioners need to help children understand rules and why they are there: they need to help children be aware of how their behaviour affects others but also help children to understand and value helping others and caring about others and foster a sense of community. This will take time and practitioners should ensure that ethos, routines and the way they enable children relate to each other, help children feel part of a caring group where everybody is important and valued.

Case study

Mikey and Joanna are both 4 and are playing together with a ball. Their play is cooperative and they are enjoying it. Sam comes along and takes the ball and starts to roll it to Mikey. He says to Mikey play with me now and so Mikey starts to play with Sam. Joanna tries to join in but they run off and exclude Joanna. She starts to cry and chases after them and pushes Sam and takes the ball. Sam goes to the practitioner and says Joanna pushed him and took his ball and it's not fair.

Reflections for career entry level

- How would you respond to Sam?
- What do you think Joanna was feeling?
- How do you think these feelings may have influenced her actions?

Reflections for leader/manager

- Are staff confident to help children manage conflict?
- In what ways do you support staff to manage behaviour?

Transition to Key Stage 1 (5 to 7 years of age)

When children move into Year 1 at 5 to 6 years old there can be many pressures on teachers to make children conform to a very different environment with much more emphasis on covering a more formal curriculum. Timetables become more formal as do ways of working and sometimes children are expected to make big adaptations with little recognition of their readiness. Teachers and parents can sometimes make assumptions about children's levels of development and experience; they may expect children to fit into their practices rather than responding to the child as an individual and supporting them appropriately. This can lead to children feeling confused and anxious, feelings they are unlikely to be able to express directly, and so can lead to inappropriate behaviour. It is important for teachers to be familiar with what children can do and support them in a sensitive manner into Key Stage 1.

Physically children are starting to develop more control but they still need opportunities to run and use their energy and to be active in their learning.

Long periods in confined spaces and limited opportunities for children to move around can be very difficult for many children and may result in poor behaviour. This may be particularly true when children are asked to sit on the carpet and concentrate without moving for 20 minutes, which can seem like a long time for many children. Children still become tired and may need time to rest and access to snacks and water. Many classes encourage access to water bottles and fruit.

At this stage teachers may expect children to have the cognitive abilities to reason and make sensible choices about behaviour and while children are starting to develop this capacity they still need help and guidance in doing this. This represents a challenge where staff: child ratios are 1:30. They may also be expected to engage in a curriculum and a way of learning which they find difficult. These may include lots of tasks sitting at tables where they are required to remember and follow instructions, organize themselves and their resources, meet time deadlines and do lots of writing. These expectations can be very daunting and where children are unable to manage the tasks they may feel angry or frustrated and this may damage their self-esteem. This may lead to children using avoidance behaviour and disrupting others. If the task itself is too difficult for the child they may feel inferior and if this happens frequently it can damage their confidence which may lead to seeing themselves as a failure. This in turn will have a negative impact on children's behaviour and their behaviour may become withdrawn or they may display behaviours teachers see as difficult such as clowning, or being disruptive or aggressive. Teachers need to be open to the idea that they can influence and mange children's behaviour by providing learning activities which are active, appropriate and accessible for children in which they can successfully engage in them. For example organizing learning through activities such as cooking, or using role play and drama techniques.

Emotionally, children are able to start to recognize their emotions and with adult help can start to describe them. They are beginning to understand that others have feelings and to empathize with others. However, they will still need adults to help them. They are starting to be able to control their feelings, for example by waiting their turn. But in some situations they may still find it difficult to control their emotions for example if they are tired or feel anxious. They still need to feel safe and valued and it is important for teachers to get to know children as individuals and respond to them in that way. This can be a challenge in a class of 30, bur if a teacher does not see this as being important then children who struggle to conform to the expectations may receive a negative response from adults and this can lead to low self-esteem.

Socially, children are starting to be able to select friends and recognize the reciprocal nature of friendship. However, this is still in its early stages and children may still find it difficult to control their own needs and feelings in response to their peers and will need support to sort out disputes. Friendships and the skills needed to form these are key social skills and where children lack these or are unable to manage their own feelings sufficiently to make or maintain friendships this may result in children feeling isolated and unhappy which in turn can lead to unacceptable behaviour. Therefore teachers need to continue to help children develop key skills of listening, self-assertion, cooperation, considering other points of view and managing conflict (Roffey, 2001).

Morally children will have much more understanding of rules and the consequences of breaking rules. They will also be increasingly able to recognize their own thoughts and feelings and be able to understand that others may also have similar thoughts and feelings. For example feelings of distress if something they value is lost or broken (Kohlberg, 1996). However they will still not be able to apply rules consistently or think through the consequences of the actions they take and how they may affect others. Teachers need to help children understand why we need rules and involve them in creating them. When children break rules they need help to discuss what happened and how it may have affected others.

Reflections for career entry professional

- How do you support children in making and maintain friendships?
- Do you help children recognize and understand other children's points of view?
- Is the timetable flexible enough to meet the needs of individual children?

Reflections for leaders/managers

- How do you plan for the transition between Foundation Stage and Key Stage 1?
- In what ways can the curriculum and the environment be adapted to meet the needs of children of 5 and 6 years old?

Managing children's behaviour

Having considered some aspects of children's development in relation to behaviour it is important for practitioners to discuss and agree how they will approach behaviour in their setting. It is essential to create a warm and caring ethos where all children are valued and helping children acquire the skills to manage their own behaviour and develop self-control is part of the learning process. This will include how the environment is organized and maintained, the rules and routines that are in place and the knowledge and skills of staff and how this influences their practice.

Enabling environments

Another of the Early Years Foundation Stage (DCSF, 2008 b) principles is about creating an enabling environment which supports young children and enables them to manage their behaviour. It is very important and practitioners should spend time planning and maintaining this. They need to think about the physical layout of the space available and how it can be best utilized to provide room for children to move around and engage in rest but also have opportunities to be more boisterous. Observing how children use the space and adapting it to the needs of different groups is essential. Practitioners need to ensure that they can see the children and also that the children can see them; this will ensure they can provide support and reassurance for children. Flexibility is important, the space should fit the children, and not the children fit the space. For example if the practitioner observes that children need opportunities for exuberant play they should support this by providing space and resources to meet this need rather than just expecting children to conform or adapt to the space provided and inhibit their behaviour.

There needs to be a range of good quality engaging resources which children can use and access easily. Limited resources mean that children will have to share or will never get access to them which will lead to feelings of frustration and even disputes and aggression which could be avoided. Poor behaviour can be the result of challenging environmental conditions rather than the function of a 'naughty child'.

The curriculum should be planned around children's needs and interests so it engages them and stimulates them, if this is the case children are less likely to become bored and behave unacceptably. They need to be active and involved in activities which will help them learn and develop physically, cognitively, socially and emotionally. They need opportunities to make choices and to become engrossed in an activity. They need to be encouraged and supported to take risks and feel successful. As it is the development of all these areas which will help them to recognize, manage and control their behaviour effectively. Poor behaviour may be a result of children being bored.

Photograph 4.2 Professional with ears, lips and eyes cards (photograph by Tracy Gannon, Headteacher, Ripley Infant School)

The environment should be planned so as to enable children to become involved with the organization and management of the setting as much as possible such as the taking out and putting away of resources, washing up, preparing and setting out snacks. This allows them to start to be in control, take some responsibility for looking after others and contributing to the community. This will help them feel they belong and foster a sense of helping others.

Task

Spend some time observing your setting and how children use it.
Consider the following questions

- Can children move freely around the setting?
- Can they easily access the resources they need?

⇨

- Which areas do children spend a lot of time in?
- Which activities do they spend time engaged in?
- Which areas do children spend very little time in?
- Which activities do children spend little time doing?
- In what ways does your setting encourage children to take responsibility for them themselves and others?

Routines and rules

Children need to feel secure and understand what is expected of them. A good way of doing this is to introduce routines which are familiar to children. Such routines will also help with the smooth management of the setting and can be a good way to help children take some control of everyday aspects of their day (Roffey, 2001). It is important to help children learn routines and practise them and while some children may take to them with ease other children will need more support and it may take longer for them to become established. Using a visual timetable can be a useful way of helping children understand the pattern of the day and act as reminder of the routines. Changes in routine can also cause children to feel unsure and even anxious and this may lead to inappropriate behaviour. So when routines have to be changed or suspended practitioners should try to warn children of the changes and give them extra support and reassurances about managing the different expectations (Mortimore, 2006).

Simple rules (few in number) which children understand and remember can help children guide their behaviour. These often relate to looking after other children, health and safety and taking care of resource. Children need to be able to understand what they mean, why they are important and how to apply them. So rules should be in child friendly language and children need to have opportunities to explore what they mean and how they may be applied in different situations through role play and stories. Even then children will not always follow them consistently, perhaps because their own emotions get the better of them or they do not know how to apply them in the particular context. When this is the case there should be discussion about what the rule is and why it's there and what the affect has been on others once it has been broken.

Case study

The children in a reception class had learned a set of routines for coming into the classroom in the morning, they knew they had to hang their coats up, put their lunch box in the container outside the classroom, change their library book in the class library with their parent or carer, put their book bag in the box and then follow the self-registration procedure by moving their name from out to in on the board and finally answer the question of the morning laid out on a table. Once they had completed all these routines they were free to choose an activity until the practitioner called the group together to start the morning. One morning the teacher was sick and a supply teacher was in the classroom, the lunch box container was not out, there were no names on the self-registration board and instead of the morning activity the children were asked to come straight to the carpet area and sit and wait until all the children arrived. Unusually five of the children found it hard to leave their mothers and started to cry. Several children started to touch and irritate other children on the carpet and one child fell over a lunch box. The supply teacher found it difficult to settle the children and start the day.

Reflections for career entry level

- What routines had the teacher set in place?
- How would these routines help the smooth transition into the classroom?

Reflections for leader/manager

- Do the routines in the setting support the children and their learning?
- How well do you prepare children for changes in routines?

Photograph 4.3 Classroom with various different areas (photograph by Emma Jordan)

Practitioners' understanding, responses and skills

Most practitioners recognize that it is important for children to be able to manage their behaviour so that they can engage effectively with the learning process and to be able to develop, build and maintain relationships. However children's behaviour and how we manage and respond to it can be challenging for many practitioners. Sometimes they feel unsure of the most effective ways of working with children to support the development of skills. In addition it can be challenging to develop sufficient understanding of children in order to help them manage their own behaviour. It may be that they are unsure how to respond to inappropriate behaviours children may display, or that practitioners feel out of control and this can lead to stress or feelings of inadequacy and sometimes even defensiveness. All these represent normal feelings in response to the complexity of managing many individuals in the context of a setting. However, there are practices which can effectively support practitioners and children (Rodd, 1996).

It is very important in all settings for the practitioners to work together to develop an approach to supporting and managing behaviour in their setting which is appropriate for their children (DCSF, 2008 b). This should include an agreed understanding of the types of behaviour they wish to see, what they agree is important in relation to helping children develop and achieve these behaviours and how they will be supported to achieve them. This would normally be in the form of a behaviour policy. A policy should represent an 'agreed' approach. It should be shared and discussed with parents and other professionals. Open discussions of this nature can help everyone understand and clarify what, why and how the setting approaches and manages behaviour. It is essential that this is based on building children's self-esteem and confidence. Central to this is developing good relationships with children and recognizing that children can learn how to manage and control their behaviour with support and help from trained and well-informed practitioners (Mortimore, 2006).

Managing children's behaviour can be emotionally, physically and intellectually demanding because of the range of different children and their variable needs. Children are all different and as such require individual responses from practitioners who have their very best interest at heart.

However it is also important to acknowledge the individuality of practitioners and so systems which enable them to share and discuss their own attitudes and values are key as these can influence their approaches. These need to be explored to fully understand how they influence us and whether they influence what we do in the best way to support and manage children's behaviour in light of current understanding of child development. For example, a practitioner may feel that shouting at a child is an effective strategy however once they realize some children experience this as aggressive and understand that it doesn't usually help children recognize what they have done wrong, they can see a reason to engage in a more suitable strategy for managing behaviour.

It is very important that practitioners understand that behaviour is learned and that they can help children learn and if necessary modify behaviour. It is not helpful to blame children for their behaviour or locate responsibility for managing it with parents. It is more useful for practitioners to have a shared approach to understanding and managing behaviour and to be open to learning more about how to prevent inappropriate behaviour through creating a supportive environment and ethos and through their own responses to children. This is not always an immediate event but a process which may take time. Sometimes it takes patience and persistence. Practitioners need to be aware of their professional responsibility to develop a repertoire of skills to manage behaviour which include being able to be calm and reassuring but firm and clear when necessary. They need to be able to be a good role model for children demonstrating good communication skills, cooperative skills and respect for colleagues. They need to have an enquiry and problem-solving approach to managing behaviour rather than just being reactive or passing the problem onto someone else.

To manage and control their own behaviour children need to understand and mange their own thoughts, feelings and actions in a range of situations and with a range of different people. Practitioners can help children explore their feelings and how these may influence their actions, and also help them recognize that other people have feelings too. They can also help children learn social skills which will support their interactions with others and help them develop and maintain relationships (sometimes referred to as emotional literacy). Stories, puppets and role play can really help children identify and explore feelings and will help children develop a vocabulary and practitioners can help children relate these to their own experiences (Swift, 2006). They may help children in rehearsing and practicing ways of behaving but children will still need support and help in applying these to different situations and contexts. For example if a visitor is invited to the classroom practitioners can rehearse with the children how to greet the visitor, practise any questions they may ask the visitor, suggest ways to thank the visitor and how to say goodbye.

Praise and rewards

A very useful strategy for managing behaviour and helping children recognize appropriate behaviour is using praise (Rogers B. M., 2008). Skinner is a behaviourist theorist who believed children are blank sheets and that they will learn how to behave through imitating those around them but also by being rewarded for good behaviour but punished for bad behaviour (Skinner, 1953). This theory has underpinned many approaches to managing behaviour in education although more recently there has been a greater focus on recognizing and rewarding positive behaviour. Rewards can take many forms including body language, smiling, positive gestures such as thumbs up, praise and tangible things such as stickers and stars.

Praise needs to be specific to the behaviour and can be accompanied by positive body language such as a smile, for example 'Well done Mikey for sitting down ready for the story'. Children do not always know what is expected in different contexts or may have become distracted or missed instructions so reminders and drawing their attention to the expected behaviour in important. In groups of young children when the practitioners focuses on the desired behaviour of a child in a positive and constructive way it often serves as a reminder for other children and they will then also display the required behaviour. This tends to have a more positive impact on children and helps them recognize what the required behaviour is in that context rather than a negative approach such as 'Joanna, you are not sitting down' in a cross tone of voice.

Some settings may use more tangible rewards such as stickers, food or objects. This needs to be very carefully thought about as there can be a danger of children not understanding how the reward relates to their behaviour and therefore being unable to recognize how their behaviour is appropriate. They may be only interested in the external reward rather than learning to gain intrinsic satisfaction and gain control over their own behaviour. There is also a danger that some children may not gain these rewards as their behaviour does not merit it and therefore further damage their self -esteem. Such approaches may be more appropriate when used within an individual behaviour plan to help encourage a specific desired behaviour and part of a planned intervention.

There are varied views in relation to the use of rewards, some people may think of them as bribery, some may consider them an appropriate and immediate way of acknowledging when a child has behaved in an appropriate and acceptable way. It is important for practitioners to discuss what they mean by rewards and what rewards they may use in their setting and how this will fit into their overall approach to behaviour management.

Consequences and sanctions

It is important for all practitioners in a setting to agree the role of consequences and sanctions in their approach to behaviour management. There are still some adults who believe that children should be punished (something the child may find distressing or disagreeable) to help them learn how to behave. However this does not necessary achieve the desired outcome and can harm children's self -esteem (Rodd, 1996). The desired outcome is for children to learn what appropriate behaviour is and be able to manage and control their behaviour themselves and not just in response to a fear of punishment. In order for children to do this they need help and support to learn what the desired behaviours are and how to apply them. When things do go wrong they need to be able to work thorough with an adult what happened, the effect it has had and how it can be resolved.

Settings can employ a hierarchy of consequences and sanctions (Rogers B., 2002) which start with ignoring or diverting inappropriate behaviour. Redirecting the child reminds children of what they are supposed to be doing; non-verbal communication can be useful here using looks and gestures such as pointing to the eyes to remind children to look or ears to listen. With these responses practitioners are helping children modify their behaviour in a positive way and giving children support rather than focusing on the negative behaviour which can sometimes make children feel inadequate and lead to behaviour deteriorating. If children do not respond to the previous approaches then a warning may be required which signals to the child their behaviour is unacceptable, this should focus on the behaviour and how it needs to be changed; it should be delivered in a firm tone of voice. If children do continue to misbehave then it is necessary to ensure they understand that their behaviour is unacceptable and teachers need to state this clearly, focusing on the behaviour, why it is unacceptable and offers an alternative. For example, 'Stop throwing the Lego, someone will get hurt. You need to finish building the house'. If children still don't respond then it may be necessary to move them away from the activity. However it is important to talk to the child about why this is happening and help them to understand how their behaviour led to this and what they could do next time so they can play acceptably with the Lego.

Time out is a sanction often used in early years settings but it is important to discuss what this means and how it will be applied. Ignoring or isolating children for long periods can be damaging for children's self- esteem. However, time separated from the group in a safe place to calm down or as a chance for children to recognize their unacceptable behaviour needs to stop can be useful. But this should be for a short period of time (no more than 5 minutes) and it is still important for adults to help child understand why their behaviour was a problem, how it affected others and how it could be changed in the future.

Children with emotional, social and behaviour issues

While most children will respond well to a carefully managed environment with practitioners who meet their needs and support their behaviour development sensitively, there will be some children who demonstrate more severe, frequent and prolonged issues such as hurting others, disrupting others, frequent tantrums or refusal to comply with adult instructions. In such cases practitioners need to consider the severity and the frequency and identify what the actual behaviours are. They may do this by observing the child and collecting information about where the behaviour occurs and how often and whether it occurs with particular individuals, practitioners or contexts. It is important that practitioners do not prejudge outcomes but use the information they collect to analyse if there are certain patterns of behaviour or triggers. They need to note what actually happened, what behaviour was displayed and what the outcomes were for the child. They should also collect information from other adults in the setting such as lunchtime supervisory staff as well as parents. With this information practitioners can work out what is actually happening rather than what they think is happening and plan support and interventions which are appropriate. These may involve changing an aspect of the environment, or the way practitioners respond to the child or helping the child learn a specific way of behaving in a certain situation. It should help adults working with the child have a more consistent approach.

Sometimes practitioners need to take extra advice or refer the child to another agency such as the SENCO, Educational Psychologist or behaviour support specialist. However this will not take away the responsibility of helping the child to manage their behaviour but it may provide more specialist information and advice.

References

Bowlby, J. (1969) *Attachment and Loss.* New York: Basic Books

DCSF (2008a) *Social and Emotional Aspects of Learning. Guidance for Practitioners Working in the Early Years Foundation Stage.* London: Department of Children, Schools and Families

DCSF (2008b) *The Early Years Foundation Stage. Practice Guidance.* London: Department of Children, Schools and Families

Erickson, E. (1963) *Childhood and Society* (2nd edition). New York: Norton

Goleman, D. (1996) *Emotional Intelligence. Why It Can Matter More Than IQ.* London: Bloomsbury

Holt, N. (2007) *Bring The Highscope Approach To Your Early Years Setting.* Abingdon: Routledge

Kohlberg, L. (1996) 'Moral stages and moralization: The cognitive developmental approach', in T. Lickona (ed.) *Moral Development and Behaviour: Theory Research and Social Issues* . New York: Holt, pp. 31–53

Lindon, J. (1997) *Working with Young Children* (3rd edition). London: Hodder and Stoughton

Maslow, A. H. (1968) *Towards a Psychology of Being.* New York: Van Nostrand

Mortimore, H. (2006) *Behaviour Management in the Early Years.* Stafford: QEd Publications

Papatheodorou, T. (2005) *Behaviour Problems in the Early Years. A Guide for Understanding and Support.* Abingdon: RoutledgeFalmer

Piaget, J. (1965) *The Moral Judgement of the Child.* New York: Free Press

Porter, L. (2003) *Young Children's Behaviour. A Practical Approach for Caregivers and Teachers.* London: Paul Chapman Publishers

Pre-school Learning Alliance (2007) *The Social Child.* London: Pre-school Learning Alliance

Rodd, J. (1996) *Understanding Young Children's Behaviour.* St Leonards: Allen & Unwin

Roffey, S. O. (2001) *Young Child Classroom Behaviour* (2nd edition). London: David Fulton Publishers

Rogers, B. (2002) *Classroom Behaviour. A Practical Guide to Effective Teaching, Behaviour Management and Colleague Support.* London: Paul Chapman Publishing

Rogers, B. M. (2008) *Behaviour Management With Young Children. Crucial First Steps with Children 3–7.* London: Sage

Skinner, B. F. (1953) *Science and Human Behaviour.* London: Macmillan

Swift, J. (2006) *Setting The Scene for Positive Behaviour in The Early Years. A Framework for Good Practice.* Abingdon: Routledge

Upton, C. a. (1992) 'An ecosystemic approach to classroom behaviour problems', in K. Wheldall (ed.) *Discipline in Schools. Psychological Perspectives on the Elton Report.* London: Routledge

Vygotsky, L. (1962) *Thought and Language.* Cambridge, MA: MIT Press

Self-Care 5

Introduction

Self-care involves children in developing increasing independence and taking responsibility for themselves, by toileting, washing, cleaning teeth, feeding, dressing themselves etc. They will develop a sense and respect for themselves (DCSF, 2008) and others. In this way, self-care involves aspects of social, emotional and physical development.

The development of self-care from birth to 3 years of age

The beginning of self-care can be seen in babies from birth, in the form of *'instinctual responses'* (Bowlby, 1958: 369), that help survival. These include, clinging, crying, smiling and following with eyes and once mobile following in actuality and have the biological function of encouraging bonding so that adults feel an emotional attachment to children and bond with them.

Indeed, babies apparently cry with the same intonation as their mother's voice in the womb (Mampe et. al., 2009) and so national and regional accents are reflected in their crying, helping them to bond quicker and be cared for more effectively. As well as bonding with their mother, father and close carers, babies may also become attached to objects, which comfort them. As children initially have a sucking reflex and are comforted by suckling, even if they are not hungry, this may be a dummy or comforter, but some children are comforted by a favourite toy or a cloth. If this attachment persists and children do not sleep without the object or a dummy, this can create problems; emotionally when the favourite toy is 'worn out' or needs washing and physically, when dummies start to affect developing teeth and corrective orthodontic treatment is needed. Joel became very attached to one soft toy that he called 'Dogger' and when his grandmother washed and recovered it, he was quite upset, as it was not his 'Dogger' anymore. Tommy had a specific toy and became very distressed if it was washed and so his mother gave his baby brother a muslin cloth as a comforter and so it was not one recognizable object. Emma was given a dummy to comfort her as she fell asleep in her cot and did not need it after the first 4 months, while her brother Drew found his thumb after 3 months and in the next 7 years caused problems with his teeth that needed braces to correct.

Babies cry for a variety of reasons, expressing hunger, discomfort, thirst, tiredness or loneliness and as they gain greater control over their bodies, they begin to move their arms and legs and point at things they want. When they drop toys out of their prams they will cry to attract attention of an adult and use their eyes to look at the toy and reach down towards it to indicate that they would like it picked up. If the 'wrong' toy is picked up the baby may change their cry, leaving no-one in doubt about what they want. When babies are weaned, they indicate that they are ready for food by opening their mouths very wide. When they want to be picked up, they may make noises and hold up their arms. At 6 months, Frank would sit quietly on the floor with his toys while his older sister played around him. He would follow her with his eyes and she would dance around him. One day his sister, who was sitting close to him on the floor, pulled on his jumper so that he lost his balance and fell backwards and started to cry. His mother came and comforted him and sat him back up again. The next day, Frank was seen pushing himself backwards and falling over and crying, so that he could be picked up and comforted.

In their second year, children become more independent and want to do things for themselves. This can be encouraged at an earlier age by giving children finger food for their tea and allowing them to feed themselves, or giving them a spoon while you are feeding them, so they can 'have a go'. This can be very messy but the children will develop fine motor skills, as well as the independence and so it is worth the mess.

Photograph 5.1 Feeding myself (© P. Hopkins)

Self-care routines are important for children in the first 3 years, so that they come to expect cleaning their teeth after meals, toileting, washing and dressing themselves. They can be encouraged to do some of this for themselves and can be given a sponge at an early age to help wash themselves in the bath, or a plastic mug to pour water over their head to get used to the water on their head. This can be part of water play at bath time and can help children to care for themselves and learn about water, bubbles, soap (see Cooper et. al., 2010). They can also be given the toothbrush to brush their own teeth or play brushing teeth of teddy. Children will also like to choose their clothes and can make some strange choices, which parents and carers would not choose. Sometimes, as they assert their independence, children will demand clothes they do not have, as I remember well from my own daughter, who one day demanded 'red knickers', which she knew she did not have. They can be encouraged to check the weather conditions and make informed choices about the warmth or waterproof needs for the day and looking through the available clothes can help them assert their independence and decision-making skills. They can also develop an awareness that their choices have consequences, so that if they choose a warm jumper on a hot day, they will feel hot and if they choose a thin T-shirt on a cold day, they may feel cold. It is good to let them come to this realization themselves, but have more appropriate clothing ready for them to change in to. Dressing teddy and dolls in clothes can give them physical skills to help develop motor skills (see Cooper and Doherty, 2010) by fitting the clothes and attempting fastenings. Some clothes are easier than others to put on, needing only pulling on without fastenings. Parents and carers can help the children dress themselves by finding some clothes that have simple fastenings initially, like Velcro and moving on to poppers and buttons and zips. Praise when children manage to put on a coat or hat by themselves will encourage them to try more complex items of clothes or fastenings. The children may need help to do some actions and it is tempting when they do the buttons up incorrectly, to redo it. Allowing children to help with these routines can take extra time in busy mornings or evenings but do pay dividends as the children become increasingly able to do things for themselves. In addition, when they go to part- or full-time care and they do not have the one-to-one attention that they may get at home, this increasing independence is helpful to both them and the professionals working in the setting.

In the first 3 years, toilet training is a major aspect of self-care. Children soon become aware if they are uncomfortable because of a full or wet nappy. They also develop an awareness that adults do not wear nappies and use the toilet and that it is more socially acceptable to do this. Toilet training can be a difficult time for many parents and children, as different children are toilet trained at an earlier or later age; boys may be later than girls as they do not appear to be as aware that they need to urinate until it is too late; larger children may find a potty is too small for them but a toilet (even with a trainer seat and step) is high and frightening. Sean was a large baby at birth (4.6 kg) and so found that potties were too big for him. He was able to urinate in the toilet at about 24 months but was over 36 months before he was able to use the toilet to defecate, because he was frightened of the toilet bowl. His parents needed to be patient and he would ask for a nappy when he needed to defecate and had to be encouraged to use the toilet and praised when he managed to do it.

When children are able to take themselves to the toilet when they need it, they also need to be able to clean themselves up and so should be encouraged to do this with their parent or carer, given some toilet paper or a moist wipe and allowed to wipe themselves.

Case study

The following are extracts from Andrea's journal of her daughter, Holly.

15 months

You really enjoy brushing your teeth and want several helpings of toothpaste. You are less keen about me brushing since you prefer chewing and sucking. You say 'tee' to indicate brushing time.

You're a good eater but you still throw food on the floor sometimes. We try to discourage this.

You have a giant open mouth like a baby bird when you want to be fed. You present it to whoever has the food you want.

16 months

You are very helpful and are getting good at following instructions. You like to put the shoes away. You passed me pegs today as I hung out the washing. You 'helped' me wash up after dinner which resulted in a lot of water everywhere.

Twice today you brought me your nappy basket to indicate that you needed to be changed. You were right both times.

You had a long play in the bath tonight. You are getting good at pouring from one cup to another. You can take off your socks and shoes but need help getting started with shirts and trousers. You like putting on my slippers and walking around.

17 months

You blow on food if it's too hot like daddy showed you.

You are consistently fetching your nappy basket when you are soiled. You know where things are and what they are for. You got out a tea bag when dad was making tea and a spoon for your yoghurt.

Tonight you got some wipes and used them to wipe the beak of our big singing duck. Then you got out the changing mat and a nappy to put on it. I had to help with putting the nappy on.

Case study—Cont'd

You used to hate having your nose wiped but you accept it now. Sometimes you request it. You've also been doing it for yourself and wiping my nose too.

You took off a t-shirt all by yourself. The socks and shoes were easy but you couldn't quite manage the trousers and nappy.

18 months

You are becoming pickier in your eating habits. You reject most vegetables now but still love fruit and grains (bread, rice, pasta). A firm 'no' is heard more often.

19 months

You enjoy mopping and sweeping. Unfortunately you crumbled some crackers on the floor so that you could sweep them up.

21 months

You are intrigued by mummy and daddy peeing. You like flushing the toilet and closing the lid. A couple of times you have got on the toilet to pee yourself but the pee was 'gone'.

You are imitating more things. You copy me washing my hands and face and drying them. The imitation is helping develop your vocabulary.

You mother your bears. You put nappies on them, feed them, give them drinks, cuddle them, sh them in the stroller and rock them to sleep.

22 months

I let you wander without a nappy for a while today. When we were upstairs you pointed to your trousers and indicated 'hot' because you were peeing. It happened again after your bath.

24 months

You are becoming more independent. You put your shoes on today and you often insist 'my turn', if we try to help you get dressed or do other things.

You were very co-operative today in brushing your teeth, washing your hair, eating dinner etc. This morning you had a dry nappy.

Soon after I changed you, you announced it was 'more nappy change' and you had another sodden nappy.

25 months

Tonight you peed in your potty. Although you've sat on the toilet before you've never actually peed. You sat on the potty several times and claimed to have peed. You then looked under the potty for the pee because it wasn't there. You were very pleased with yourself when it finally was there.

26 months

The potty training is going well, especially at the childminder's. At home you like being nappy-less but are less interested in the potty. Tonight you used the toilet.

You usually stay dry when asleep and we're gradually making progress in the day.

The potty training continues slowly. You are happy to sit on the potty or toilet but rarely manage to pee there. The laundry has increased due to your various accidents.

27 months

We had a good potty night. You did a poo in the potty for the first time. You are getting better at recognising when you need to pee.

You like to be 'naked girl'. This makes using the potty easier and keeps you cooler at night.

The potty training is going well. You've had several accident free days and are getting good at asking for the potty when you need it. You are able to walk up shallow stairs one foot per step without holding on.

28 months

You spent the morning being naked girl. The potty training is going well.

Your tummy was hurting when you woke up and you tried, unsuccessfully, to poo several times. You later managed this in your pants. Later I was talking on the phone to Auntie Robin when you said you needed the toilet. I suggested you used the potty but you declined. Instead you had a poo in the garden followed by more on the potty.

Case study—Cont'd

29 months

You are taking yourself to the toilet quite reliably. The potty is now shunned. You wanted to leave your pants on tonight so I'm going to risk the bed (with a towel). You and the bed were dry in the morning.

30 months

You asked to have a shower with me rather than your bath. You like the shower as long as there's no hair washing. The water tickles your hands and tummy and you stick your tongue in it.

I bought a squirt bottle of de-tangler for you. It does help. You prefer to use it on me and brush my hair.

You chose to wear a nappy to bed tonight although you've been out of them for a month.

31 months

You are getting better at dressing yourself. This is only possible when we're not in a hurry.

32 months

You have been helping me by doing jobs. You washed some dishes and folded some laundry and helped wrap presents. Your help creates mess.

33 months

We played with toys this evening. You used your tools to do some fixing. You made dinner with some bowls. You fed, nappied, cuddled and tucked in your bears and dolls. You put me and your people to bed and read us some stories. You had to get a blanket for your baby so he would be 'cosy and warm'.

You've been a big girl tonight, putting on your own pyjamas and peeling your own orange. You then gave some of the orange to the nasty witches and nasty monsters. Later you held their hands as we went up to bed.

You took yourself off to the toilet when we were visiting K&B but you had not left quite enough time for the journey and pulling down your tights with a resulting puddle in front of the toilet. This really upset you and we had to go home.

34 months

You tell me quite often that you are 'growing up'. Today you were explaining that you don't use nappies or a potty any more because they are for babies and you are growing up so you use the toilet. You then said that you couldn't reach the light but you would be able to soon because you're growing up.

35 months

We washed your hair in the sink today. It helped keep the water out of your eyes but you still did not enjoy the process.

Reflection for early career professional

There are a number of strands in this case study; Holly's ability to dress herself and make choices, her involvement in her own and the family's hygiene routines and her toilet training. Choose one of these strands and consider how Holly could be supported in this area at different ages?

Reflection for leader/manager

Choose one of the strands in this case study:

- the ability to dress and make choices,
- involvement in the child's own and the family's hygiene routines,
- toilet training.
- How do you support children in this area in your setting?

There are cultural differences in expectations for children's independence in self-care. In some cultures, children are not encouraged to be independent in their self-care and have adults who take responsibility for every aspect of their self-care. For example, in Brazil children in all but the poorest families will have nannies in their earliest years and in early years settings, whose responsibility it is to ensure children clean their teeth after eating, clean after toileting and do much of this care for them by washing their hands and wiping noses and bottoms. Contrast this with early years settings in the United

Kingdom where children may be given a tissue to wipe their own noses and are expected and encouraged to put the dirty tissue in the waste bin after use, or where children will take themselves to the toilet and only ask for help if they cannot manage to wipe their own bottom.

The development of self-care from 3 to 5 years of age

By the time they are 3 years of age, children will be much more independent in their self-care and are increasingly likely to attend playgroups, nurseries or other early years settings either part- or full-time. They will be able to make simple decisions about what activity they want to do and how to do it and so much of what they are engaged in is self-initiated. Both at home and in settings, children who have a wide range of toys and experiences may find the choice overwhelming and so it is often good to rotate the available toys for children so that they can choose what to play with from a limited range. The children may often use the toys available in ways that are unexpected, especially if the toys are not too specific and provide opportunities for imagination (see Johnston and Nahmad-Williams, 2010). Some experiences should be problems for them to solve (Johnston, 2005), creative activities (see Compton et al., 2010) involving designing and making (see Cooper et. al., 2010) and they should be encouraged to do these themselves and take a pride in the results. Children who have managed to dress a doll and fasten the buttons, or make a birthday card, or make a sail boat or a plasticine boat, will have a huge sense

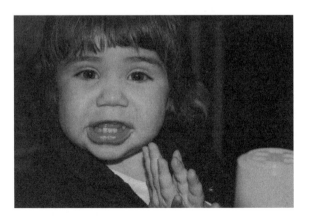

Photograph 5.2 A sense of achievement (© P. Hopkins)

of achievement and learn about the world around them, as well as develop independence and decision-making skills.

Many features of self-care are embedded in the ideas and practices of theorists. For example, the importance of daily routines is a central feature of Steiner education (Steiner, 1996), Froebel (1826) and Piaget (1950) advocated active learning and Vygotsky. Vygotsky and Cole (1978) identified how adults could support children through adult-child interaction. These ideas have been incorporated into the High/Scope Cognitively Orientated Curriculum developed by David Weikart in 1962, for children aged 3 and 4 years old. High/Scope is popular in early years settings, as it helps children to become independent and make their own decisions about activities and even to evaluate their own learning. The High/Scope curriculum is a coordinated set of ideas and practices based on the belief that children are active and independent learners, learning from activities that they plan and execute themselves (Hohmann and Weikart, 2002). Research carried out by the High/Scope Foundation into the effects of the programme on short- and long-term development indicates the positive long-term effects of children becoming independent learners, to take responsibility for their actions and self-care (Schwienhart et al., 1993).

By the time children reach the end of the Early Years Foundation Stage, they will be aware if the social and health reasons for personal hygiene and take responsibility for their own care. In settings they should be able to mange their own toilet, recognize the need to wash their hands, blow their noses, sneeze into a handkerchief and dispose of dirty tissues. They should be able to undress for physical exercise and dress again afterwards. They should be able to put their coats, hats, gloves and boots on by themselves for outside play in wet or cold weather and sun hats in warm weather and put on outside wear at the end of the setting session.

Case study

The following are further extracts from Andrea's journal of her daughter, Holly.

36 months

You've started to wipe your own bottom. You've been sharing your toys and time quite well with Ben when they are his toys but less well

Case study—Cont'd

when they are your toys. You did save some sweeties to offer him though.

37 months

You've been practising tying knots tonight. They don't always work but we've established a procedure that works most of the time.

You have a doll or bear asleep in your bed most of the time. You have been very good recently about going to sleep in your own bed after a few stories. You still wake up in the night and join us sometimes.

You have worked out how to jump onto your swing when it's pushed back so that you can start swinging without needing a push.

You started at a day nursery today. Dad took you up and stayed with you for a while but you settled in quickly and were quite happy to be left with the other children. You didn't eat much but did try the vegetable soup.

38 months

You are getting better about playing by yourself while dad does some work.

We talked about eating lunch at the nursery. You agreed to try to eat some. This was made easier by the fact they were serving spaghetti. The nursery staff said you are better if they feed you.

You approved of the nursery food today, even though it was new to you. It was toad in the hole with carrots and apparently you ate it all up. You ate a lot in the evening again. I think a growth spurt may be looming.

You want to wear the same sort of clothes as me some days. Today you wanted to wear a pretty dress because I put one on. Later when I was changing out of my work clothes you wanted to put on your cow t-shirt because I put on my cow sweatshirt. Dad brought us matching shirts from his trip to Spain and you really like those.

You are capable of feeding yourself but you often prefer to be fed. You will generally start a meal feeding yourself but then demand that we feed you. At nursery you are capable of wiping yourself after going to the toilet but at home you prefer to have this service performed for you.

39 months

You were helping dad sweep the steps when I got home and were very proud that you had been helping to clean up. You helped me plant some seedlings in the garden. You like to use your own tools.

40 months

You made me be a baby again today. Most of what you say as a mummy is a reflection of things Paul and I say to you. You are very reassuring to your baby. You've been talking about things you did when you were a little baby. Sometimes they are baby things and sometimes they are just a few months ago.

Bed time is turning into more of a battle. You drag your feet at every point and try to delay the process. We use number of stories as an incentive. You were so obstreperous tonight that you dropped to no stories. This led to hysterics. I allowed you to earn a story back by getting into bed and lying calmly for two minutes. This worked.

You are very fond of ice cream. We've been buying boxes of ice lollies and you have one most days. You've been very good about asking permission before helping yourself to one from the freezer.

41 months

You were being self-righteous when you came home from nursery today. You hadn't needed your mummy, unlike Bridget who had cried and you hadn't been silly with your tea, unlike some of the other children.

Recently you've been deciding that you don't have enough breath to do things. This includes not being able to go to sleep. We have to blow into your mouth to donate breath which then travels down your body to your toes. You sometimes return the breath later.

Today was your first day of school. Dad and I both took you and then dad stayed with you for a bit but you told him to leave. You recognised your name card and then were able to find your peg. You have the sandcastle peg. You told me that you did everything the teacher asked.

42 months

I took you to school this morning. You know the routines well and were able to show me what to do. You sat down confidently on the carpet and I didn't even get a good-bye.

Case study—Cont'd

You told daddy you were his wife and you had to do lots of vacuuming because you were his wife. This is odd since daddy does most of the vacuuming. How quickly stereotypes can develop.

We had our first major confrontation today. You were being mildly unco-operative through the evening and striking out at dad and I but then you consistently refused to pick up some food you had spilled. The end result was denial of privileges for tomorrow and many tears before bedtime. The next day you appeared to survive the 'no treat' day with some understanding. We did need to keep reminding you about why there were no treats and how to earn them back.

Dad took you to the Health Visitor for your check up and booster shots. You were very good and just closed your eyes for the injections but didn't cry or squirm.

43 months

You burnt your fingers on the stove. Dad had told you not to touch the burner but you touched it deliberately. Luckily it was on low.

Most days you request a pretty dress rather than trousers. You really prefer ones that spin well – the grey dress is the best for that. You are very girly in some ways and are keen to identify with me and other 'girls'. Pink has become your favourite colour.

44 months

You and Lucy bumped heads today at nursery. According to you, you were very brave and didn't cry but Lucy cried and cried and cried. You put a lot of importance on being big. It bothers you that Bobbie is slightly taller and slightly older than you. When you make me be the baby I have to be smaller than you.

Gender issues kept arising today. You would hold mummy's hand because we were both girls. You sat on a sofa with me because it was the girls' sofa and daddy was on the boys' sofa. You also announced that you and Tom from nursery were going to get married because boys and girls marry each other.

45 months

You were not playing nicely this evening so we had to stop. You kept changing the order of play and refusing to take your turn. At bed time you wanted some 'read it yourself' books. You've been 'reading' Puss and Boots to yourself after your story allocation has been used up.

Reflection for early career professional

- What are the main features of Holly's development of self-care in this extract?
- What are the main challenges in the development of self-care for Holly and her carers at this age?
- How could Holly's carers support her development in self-care?

Reflection for leader/manager

- How does your setting support children at this age in caring for themselves?
- How can your setting support children in becoming independent and making decisions for themselves?
- What are the challenges to supporting self-care in the 3- to 5-year olds? How can you overcome these challenges?

Transition to Key Stage 1 (5 to 7 years of age)

The biggest challenge for children is the move from a personalized, skills-based curriculum in the Early Years Foundation Stage (DCSF, 2008) to a more general subject and cognitive-based curriculum in Key Stage 1 (DfEE, 1999). In the National Curriculum, self-care is a small part of Personal Social and Health Education (PSHE) which is not a subject in itself. Indeed, there have been concerns expressed in the Cambridge Review (Alexander, 2009) about the lack of focus in primary education on wider social development.

Some Key Stage 1 settings have also expressed concern about the widening gap between children who enter their settings. Some children are unable to care for themselves and are not well toilet trained or may not be able to dress themselves, while other children may have a highly developed independence and are used to making their own decisions, which the environment of the setting does not build upon. Key Stage 1 teachers are often not equipped to support development in self-care. This may be because:

- children may enter KS1 with a vast range of abilities, with some able to care for themselves and others who need considerable support. Since class size is up to thirty at KS1 and teachers may have little additional adult support, this can make undressing for and dressing after PE very time-consuming. If children need to be helped to clean themselves after toileting, this may require specialized support, difficult if there is not additional support and you have to wait for another adult to arrive to help out.
- teachers at KS1 are 'trained' to focus on narrow educational targets, the outcomes of which they are 'judged' by. This makes it difficult to support children in aspects of social and personal development, when the emphasis is on raising standards of literacy and numeracy. PSHE is often developed as separate sessions or during circle time (see Mosely, 2009) rather than as part of role play, which can support children in aspects of self-care (see Johnston and Nahmad-Williams, 2010).
- children may have a well-developed independence from their experiences in the Early Years Foundation Stage and the transition from child to teacher-led activities can present problems for both children and teachers. Children may be used to making their own decisions about what they do and how they do it and teachers may have expectations of greater control.

A recent observation of Year 2 children, many of whom had special educational needs such as autism and Asperger's syndrome, showed, with some clarity, that children who are allowed greater independence also manage their own learning better. The children took greater care of themselves and others, were fully engaged in the learning and there were no behaviour problems. This indicates that teachers will have greater control over the behaviour and learning of children, if they are less controlling of them. It also indicates that learning activities (even those with a cognitive focus) can address issues of social development and self-care. Other, more play-based, activities can allow children to address issues of self-care in play contexts while they are developing other areas of learning.

Supporting the development of self-care

Children learn about self-care by being given opportunities:

- to learn by imitation,
- to follow routines,
- to make decisions for themselves and learn from their experiences,
- to explore self-care issues in role-play activities,
- to discuss with others issues that they are struggling to address.

They will also develop best through modelling, praise and encouragement, rather than criticism and being left alone to fail. This can occur in an Enabling Environment (DCSF, 2008) which provides a key person for children to relate to, allows them to focus on activities that stem from their own interests and needs and addresses specific religious and cultural aspects of self-care. For example, children may play as washing themselves in preparation or covering their head before prayer.

Photograph 5.3 Role play that develops self-care (Photography by L. Nahmad-Williams)

Practical task – using the role-play area for self-care

Set up the role-play area as a home corner, with a bed, dressing table, box or hanger with clothes, shoes and hats. If the area can be set up close to a sink or a bathroom, the play can involve bathing, washing etc. Children can be provided with their own

Case study—Cont'd

toothbrush or bring a wash bag from home with some items like a toothbrush, flannel, hair brush etc.

Children can wash, clean their teeth and brush their hair (either for real or in imaginary play). They can dress themselves and toy dolls and each other. If you have bathing facilities, children can have a bubble bath and wash and play in the bath and then dry and dress themselves.

Listen to the children as they play and interact with them as appropriate, questioning them about what they are doing and why.

Reflection for early career professional

- How has the activity supported understanding and skills of self-care?
- What other role-play activities can support the development of self-care? How?
- How else can you support the children in different aspects of self-care?

Reflection for leader/manager

Try out the activity with different children in your setting. With your colleagues consider,

- How has the activity supported understanding and skills of self-care in children of different ages in your setting?
- Undertake an audit to see how self-care is developed in your setting. Consider with your staff how other experiences and activities can support the development of self-care?
- How can you support children in becoming independent learners in your setting?

References

Alexander, R. (ed.) (2009) *Children, their World, their Education: Final Report and Recommendations of the Cambridge Review.* London: Routledge

Bowlby, J. (1958) 'The nature of a child's tie to his mother. *International Journal of Psychoanalysis*, 39, 350–373

Compton, A., Johnston, J., Nahmad-Williams, L. and Taylor, K. (2010) *Creative Development.* London: Continuum

Cooper, L. and Doherty, J. (2010) *Physical Development*. London: Continuum

Cooper, L., Johnston, J., Rotchell, E. and Woolley, R. (2010) *Knowledge and Understanding of the World*. London: Continuum

DCSF, (2008) *The Early Years Foundation Stage; Setting the Standard for Learning, Development and Care for Children from Birth to Five; Practice Guidance*. London: DCSF

DfEE, (1999) *The National Curriculum: Handbook for Teachers in England*. London: DfEE/QCA

Froebel, F. (1826) *On the Education of Man*. Keilhau, Leipzig: Wienbrach

Hohmann, M. and Weikart, D. P. (2002) *Educating Young Children* (2nd edition). Ypsilanti, MI: High/Scope Press

Johnston, J. (2005) *Early Explorations in Science* (2nd edition). Maidenhead: Open University Press

Johnston, J. and Nahmad-Williams, L. (2010) 'Developing imagination and imaginative play', in A. Compton, J. Johnston, L. Nahmad-Williams and K. Taylor (eds) *Creative Development*. London: Continuum

Mampe, B., Friederici, A. D., Christophe, A. and Wermke K. (2009) 'Newborns' cry melody is shaped by their native language'. *Current Biology*. http://www.cell.com/current-biology/home accessed 5/11/09

Mosely, J. (2009) Circle Time. http://www.circle-time.co.uk/ accessed 20/11/09

Piaget, J. (1950) *The Psychology of Intelligence*. London: Routledge and Kegan Paul

Schwienhart, L. J., Weikart, D. P. and Toderan, R. (1993) *High Quality Preschool Programs Found to Improve Adult Status*. Ypsilante, MI: High/Scope Foundation

Steiner, R. (1996) *The Education of the Child and Early Lectures on Education*. New York: Anthroposophic Press

Vygotsky, L. and Cole, M. (ed.) (1978) *Mind in Society, The Development of Higher Psychological Processes*. Cambridge, Mass: Harvard University Press

6 Sense of Community

Introduction

This chapter explores how children's sense of their own needs develops in the early years, and how this comes to involve the need to feel valued and accepted by others. It considers how children grow to appreciate difference, including differences relating to age, gender, ethnicity, religion and belief, disability and sexuality. It is important that children feel that their own views and feelings are valued and they are enabled to express these. This is a part of developing a positive self-image and developing self-confidence and self-esteem. However, it is also important to appreciate that others have different outlooks and feelings. This chapter uses practical examples to consider how children can be encouraged to explore and appreciate difference. It considers how education providers can avoid stereotyping through their expectations, language, and their provision and organization of resources.

Settings which appear to lack diversity, and which may be termed as mono-cultural, need to consider how they can reflect the diversity of contemporary society and provide rich experiences to help children appreciate the wider world. This chapter explores the use of visits, visitors, artefacts, stories and food to broaden children's cultural experiences; it considers the importance of a multi-sensory approach and the use of experiential learning. It also considers how parents and carers may respond to such activities and offers positive strategies to help to involve them in their children's learning. The Early Learning Goals (DCSF, 2008a) suggest that children should have a developing respect for 'their own' cultures and beliefs. This is an interesting concept, and most probably relates to developing respect for the culture and beliefs of their parents/carers or wider family. Essentially, this involves appreciating the range of backgrounds that children come from and valuing these in the setting where learning takes place. Developing links between the setting and parents/carers is an important part of modelling good relationships to children and developing a sense of community.

Appreciating difference and diversity

Appreciating difference is one of the most important things we can help children to learn. Whatever our role, we are all very aware that all people are unique and different and this is apparent from birth. Every one of us develops in different ways and at different rates, we each have our own preferences, likes and dislikes and no one else in the whole world is quite like us. As professionals we are in the privileged position of helping children to understand that they are unique and special, valued and valuable. Knowing this is a part of developing a positive self-image and developing self-confidence and self-esteem, it is also fundamental to developing self-confidence and self-assurance (as was considered in Chapter 2).

Children encounter difference in a wide range of ways from the earliest years. They see that others have different coloured hair and eyes, that they enjoy different toys and games, that some children are shy and others outgoing, that we use different words and speak in different ways, that our skin, height and weight can be different. From early in life children begin to learn about gender differences and may be treated differently because of their sex. Boys may be regarded as being boisterous, confident or brave; girls may be regarded as being kind, sweet, gentle and beautiful. As professionals we are aware of the need to give children a range of experiences and not to stereotype them according to traditional gender or other roles. Seeing each child as a unique individual is important in allowing them to develop in their own way and to find their own personality and sense of self. In addition, we need to acknowledge that each carer, parent and professional is unique and has their own needs, interests and personality.

Developing a sense of community from birth to 3 years of age

In their first year children are continually responding to their environment, appreciating differences and showing interest. Responding to touch and to facial expressions from adults, enjoying being tickled and cuddled and discovering different tastes and textures all add to the excitement of finding out about the world. During this phase it is important for adults to talk with babies, to share information and to describe what they can see, to ask questions and to tell them what they think about different people and situations. For example, 'You love Aunt Jess don't you, she always gives you hugs,' and 'Look at the ducks! Isn't it lovely how they swim on the water?' Providing children with an opportunity to see new places beyond their immediate environment provides an important stimulus: a visit to the local park or being able to sit and watch the world through the window both help babies to see people and things beyond their immediate surroundings. All this helps children to engage with their environment and to begin to develop a sense of community.

From around 8 months children increasingly understand that their actions and voices have an effect on others. They are able to show their interest in activities and benefit from others appreciating this response. They also benefit from emotional cues given by adults that show how to respond to an unfamiliar dismaying or pleasurable situation. As they begin to crawl (at around 6 months) and walk (at around 12 months) they will often glance back to their caregiver checking for a signal regarding a new toy, activity or playmate. This *social referencing* supports the child as they try new experiences (Berger, 2000). A common example is found at meal times, when parents make sounds to infer that food will taste lovely, smack their lips and pretend to try some.

From 16–26 months children are able to begin to distinguish between themselves and others and to appreciate that they are similar to, and different from, those around them (Lindon, 1993; DCSF, 2008a). During this time it is appropriate to help children become familiar with difference through picture books, photographs and by meeting other children. Introducing them to positive images of those from different cultural backgrounds, with different ethnicities and disabilities helps to promote an anti-bias and non-discriminatory approach to their learning and development.

From 22 months until the age of 3 years children are developing a much stronger sense of community including appreciating membership of their family or setting. It is important to talk with children about the special people in their lives and they will enjoy collecting pictures and photographs of friends, family members or pets. It is important to observe how children at this age show affection to the special people in their lives and to support them when they show concern for others. Piaget noted that children at this age see things from their own perspective and have difficulty in seeing things from others' viewpoints (Piaget and Inhelder, 1969). Much of their conversation is egocentric, although some talk is social communication (Thomas, 2005). Vygotsky suggested that such egocentric speech is an important tool in seeking and planning a solution to problems faced by the child, rather than being a simple accompaniment or 'sound track' to activity (Vygotsky, 1962). Selman (1980) suggested that a child's perspective was egocentric until the age of 6 and becomes more social-informational from 6–8 years, extending the ideas presented by Piaget and Vygotsky.

Case study

Simon, Joanna and Stuart are aged between 26 and 30 months and all attend the same child-minder 4 days each week. Stuart has only recently joined the group and is slowly settling into his new routine and beginning to make friends with the others. Liz, the child-minder, wants to help Stuart to settle more effectively and has decided to make collages with the children showing the activities they share together. Using a child-friendly digital camera, the children record the different places that they visit during the week by photographing each other. With Liz's help they collect images of

Case study—Cont'd

a visit to the park, a shopping trip to the baker, the green grocer and the supermarket and their weekly visit to the ball pool at the local sports' centre. They take turns photographing each other and Liz takes some extra pictures showing all three children together on each outing. Having printed three sets of photographs, the children choose their personal favourites and make a collage on a large piece of cardboard adding drawings and sticking paper shapes to add additional colour. At the end of the week each child took their poster home to show how much they had enjoyed their time together. Stuart had chosen to include photographs showing him with both Joanna and Simon and had drawn smiley faces in the spaces in-between the images. Liz chose some of the photographs showing all three children together and framed them to keep in the setting.

Photograph 6.1 Caring for the environment (© P. Hopkins)

Reflection for early career professional

- How do you think the age and maturity of the children might impact on their involvement in this activity?

- How could you extend the activity to further reinforce the sense of community shared by the children?
- Do you feel that this is an age-appropriate use of technology? What benefits does the technology bring to the process?

Reflection for leader/manager

- What strategies do you encourage professionals to use to help integrate children new to your setting?
- How do you encourage the use of technology to engage children? How do you ensure that technology is used to support collaborative learning rather than to dominate it?
- How do you encourage professionals to use the local environment and community as a learning resource? How do you balance health and safety requirements and learning opportunities to encourage a sense of community?

Developing a sense of community from 3 to 5 years of age

From 3–5 years of age it is important to enable children to share experiences from different parts of their lives with each other. They begin to make greater connections between the various spheres in which they experience friendships or acquaintances appreciating, for example, that Mrs Brook who works in the supermarket also lives in the house opposite them. The opportunity to meet different members of the community in the setting, for example the person who provides the school crossing patrol, a local police officer or fire safety officer enables children to begin to form positive relationships with people who help.

From 40 months–5 years children need to develop further their positive self-image and to feel comfortable with themselves and their sense of identity. They will have an increasing awareness of different cultures and beliefs. Taking time in the setting to celebrate special times of year from different cultures will reinforce children's experience of their own background and introduce them to new ones enjoyed by others (as discussed in Chapter 6 of

Knowledge and Understanding of the World in this series). Talk about differences and similarities can help in the appreciation of others and professionals need to be sensitive to any negative comments or attitudes and work to help children to value difference as being positive. While curiosity and enthusiasm can make this a time of great learning, it is also important to make sure that children have opportunities to be calm and tranquil, to focus on themselves and their own inner-being and to find a sense of peace. Professionals can make sure that non-discriminatory practices are modelled and valued by helping all children in a setting to participate in activities and encouraging turn-taking and listening to one another.

Case study

James and his mum are leaving the supermarket. A woman is unlocking her car to load her shopping onto the back seat. James stops and watches with fascination. 'Why doesn't she get her hands dirty?' he asks. His mum asks what he means and he replies, 'When she pushes her wheelchair doesn't she get all the dirt and wet from the tyres on her hands?' Mum takes James over to ask the lady the question, and they discover the answer together. Although he is too shy to ask the question directly himself, he discovers that each wheel has an extra rim that is used to propel the wheelchair without the need to touch the tyres. James is excited by this discovery and is really pleased that the woman will not get her hands dirty. In nursery the next day he draws a picture of the woman and uses it to explain to everyone else what he has learned.

Reflection for early career professional

- How would you use James's experience and enthusiasm to help other children to appreciate difference?
- What representations of people with different abilities and needs are available in your setting? Have you ever used stories or pictures of people with disabilities with your children?
- How can you include examples of people with disabilities in activities without always focusing on the disability?

Reflection for leader/manager

- How do you monitor the effective implementation of disability anti-discrimination legislation in your setting?

- How do you support the professionals in you setting to encourage the positive representation and inclusion of people with diverse abilities?
- What strategies do you use to ensure that charity-related fundraising activities in you setting do not reinforce negative stereotypes of people with diverse needs as being dependent or 'needy'?

Transition to Key Stage 1 (5 to 7 years of age)

Ensuring smooth progression from the Early Years Foundation Stage into Key Stage 1 can be attained through effective communication between professionals. While teachers and other staff will be familiar with curriculum and assessment arrangements in the two stages and will share children's profiles, it is also important to consider the other factors which affect a child's development and well-being.

When considering a sense of community it is key to consider how routines and activities in the two stages can be maintained during the time of transition and to support children so that they can face any difference or change confidently. Being aware of children's friendship groups, and tensions between children or families and any significant events that have impacted on valuing diversity and inclusion may help the teacher in Key Stage 1 to plan a safe, secure and welcoming environment. Transition may, in itself, provide an excellent opportunity to foster a sense of community if the children move to the new setting together and can be encouraged to support one another. It is important to help children at this age to feel a sense of pride in their own identity and that their social and cultural background is valued (Lindon, 1993).

Case study

Alojzy is 5 years old and has arrived for a first visit to a Year 1 class in preparation for starting school in a week's time. His father has been working in the local agricultural industry for the past 8 months and now the rest of the family have come to join him ⇨

Case study—Cont'd

in the United Kingdom. His mother does not speak any English but his father has been attending classes at the local College for the past 2 months. Alojzy has two older sisters who will be joining classes in Years 4 and 6. Dad explains that Alojzy loves to play football at every opportunity, likes to paint and draw and spends any spare time playing games on his computer. They have a small selection of work from his previous setting in Poland that shows evidence of well-developed fine motor skills, including pencil control and consistent letter formation and a knowledge of number bonds to 20, two-dimensional shapes and non-standard units of measure. Dad says that Alojzy is a very friendly boy who has a great deal of energy and loves to play team games.

Reflection for early career professional

- How would you support Alojzy in his first days in your setting? What are the most immediate challenges that he will face?
- How can you foster a sense of community and belonging for him and his family?
- If you were working in a setting where no other children have English as an additional language (EAL) how could you use this opportunity to promote the valuing of difference and to broaden the children's knowledge of other cultures and backgrounds?

Reflection for leader/manager

- Evaluate the policies in your setting that support inclusion and value diversity. How do the policies relate to one another? How do you monitor their effectiveness?
- What training is provided for professionals to ensure that they are familiar with and confident in the delivery of non-discriminatory practice? How do you know that policies are being implemented in an effective way?
- How is the inclusive ethos of your setting communicated to parents and carers? How do you encourage them to value difference and to promote such values with their children?

When considering a sense of community is it important not to limit what the term community means. Some children will be part of an extended family based in one locality, others will have friends and relatives based around the country or in other countries, some children will have a greater sense of other locations and countries than others. Some will be fascinated by different places and feel a connectedness with them and some children will have a link with somewhere that they lived before moving to our setting.

Many of these aspects reflect the Early Learning Goals (DCSF, 2008a: 12) that I identify as being particularly relevant to children's development of a sense of community, namely to:

- have a developing awareness of their own needs, views and feelings, and be sensitive to the needs, views and feelings of others;
- have a developing respect for their own cultures and beliefs and those of other people;
- understand that people have different needs, views, cultures and beliefs, that need to be treated with respect; and
- understand that they can expect others to treat their needs, views and cultures and beliefs with respect.

For some children, their experience will be more limited. While some settings will be very obviously diverse others may be described as mono-cultural, that is being made up of people from background and cultures that appear to be very similar. Whether our setting is multi-cultural or mono-cultural we need to consider how wider society is represented, reflected and appreciated.

Reflecting the diversity of society

Settings are not necessarily in the business of introducing children to the diversity of society: many children already live in a diverse society and experience it through personal relationships and a range of media. One only has to monitor the content of daytime television and children's programming to identify the range of differences with which children come into contact. Children are also privy to the views and attitudes of parents and carers towards such diversity and may pick up on different views and responses and replicate these in their own words and behaviour. Sometimes these may show themselves in inappropriate or seemingly intolerant ways in our settings and we will have to explain to children what our expectations for them are when they are in our setting.

Some settings that appear to lack diversity (particularly in terms of ethnicity, culture and religion) may be termed as mono-cultural. As professionals we need to consider how they can come to reflect the diversity of contemporary society and provide rich experiences to help children appreciate the wider world. Strategies to support this approach include:

- using stories and songs from different cultures and countries;
- including people from different cultural backgrounds and of different ethnicities in displays;
- considering where our food, clothes and other goods come from and appreciating our dependence on people in a wide range of localities;
- including clothing and artefacts from a variety of cultures in a role-play area and giving children background information about their origins and use;
- inviting visitors to share elements of their culture (e.g. celebrations, food, customs, clothing, stories) with the children;
- choosing media resources (television programmes, interactive software) that reflect a diverse society; and
- including diversity elements in a topic being undertaken by the children, or introducing periodic focus weeks.

Developing these strategies needs to be a part of an ongoing programme of appreciating diversity in any setting, which is a part of a wider ethos and mission, in order that activities are not isolated, disjoined or tokenistic. It is important that professionals work together to understand the purpose and importance of such activities and to feel a sense of ownership for developing the children's experience and learning. Policies relating to inclusion, diversity and equalities will be a useful point of reference for professionals and will help parents and carers to appreciate the intentions and values of the setting.

Using stories and picture books provides one way to introduce children to diverse groups of people. An excellent picture book that shows a wide variety of people from different family backgrounds, cultures and abilities is *Picnic in the Park* (Griffiths and Pilgrim, 2007) which outlines the celebration of Jason's fifth birthday and all the guests that come to help him celebrate. It is particularly useful as it is based in an experience familiar to most children, celebrating a birthday, while also introducing elements that may be new to them. Other picture books showing a wide range of diverse families are included in the *Family Diversities Reading Resource* (Morris and Woolley, 2008) available online: www.bishopg.ac.uk/fdrr.

Practical tasks

Plan a visit to your setting by a representative from the local community. Consider what learning outcomes you intend to achieve from the visit and how you will evaluate its effectiveness.

Evaluate the visit to identify how successful it was in:

- developing children's understanding of people's roles in the community;
- building trust with and respect for a responsible adult with whom the children were not already very familiar;
- fostering an appreciation of those we rely on for help and support.

Plan to follow up the visit with role-play activities, costumes, puppets or a small world activity. Observe and evaluate the children's engagement with this activity to assess their knowledge and understanding.

Developing a sense of a child's own culture and beliefs

The Early Leaning Goals (DCSF, 2008a) suggest that by the end of the EYFS children should have an appreciation of their own cultures and beliefs and be able to respect and appreciate those of others. These are interesting concepts that require careful reflection by professionals. By 'their own' culture we would seem to be considering the culture, beliefs and values of the child's family and to be seeking to reinforce these in the setting.

This area could be problematic. If a child comes from a religious background we may wish to consider how appropriate it is for a professional in a setting to seek to reinforce the particular beliefs of the family. For example, if a child comes from a family of practising Christians this, in itself, does not define what parents may believe. They may believe that the world was literally created in 6 days or may believe in a theory of evolution. They may engage in the practice of praying to the saints for guidance and support or may belong to a church denomination that does not find this useful or appropriate. Religious groups are diverse and varied, even within one religion. In addition, it is not appropriate for professionals to indoctrinate children and tell them what to believe. Our role as professionals is to provide opportunities for discovery, enquiry-based learning and to nurture the skills of reflection and questioning.

What, then is involved in developing a sense of community which addresses beliefs and values? I suggest that this involves the socialization of children so that they are able to engage with others in respectful, considerate, appreciative and inclusive ways. These will reflect and complement many of the religious and cultural beliefs of children's families. Such attributes will include:

- Care
- Patience
- Respect
- Empathy
- Patience
- Thankfulness
- Appreciation
- Listening
- Questioning
- Mutual understanding

Some children will talk to God or say prayers and find support and comfort in this. They may feel that Jesus is with them at all times as a friend or believe that Mohammed (peace be upon him) is Allah's special messenger. As professionals, our role is to appreciate the child's beliefs and the views of their

Photograph 6.2 Learning about Judaism (photograph by Emma Jordan)

parents and carers without seeking either to promote or to undermine such views. It is not our role to impose our personal views or beliefs on others (Woolley, 2010).

Considering cultural differences may be easier. Celebrating differences in the way we dress, the food we enjoy, the ways in which we mark special occasions and our daily routines can provide rich and varied experiences for children to share. While some of these may be rooted in religion they can focus more on practice and experience and provide multi-sensory encounters. Research shows that an effective way to reduce prejudice is through inter-group contact and that classrooms that expose children to ethnic diversity and that encourage children to value and understand difference prevent children from forming early negative biases (Berk, 2006).

When considering belief and culture it is important to have developed effective relationships with parents and carers. We need to be aware of any particular issues that they wish us to consider as a part of their child's learning. It may be that their beliefs mean that they do not watch television (e.g. some members of the Plymouth Brethren) or do not give gifts at Christmas or for birthdays (e.g. many Jehovah's Witnesses). The particular needs of families may vary even within particular faith groups and we need to be willing to ask questions and to seek guidance from parents and carers in particular situations. We can then be respectful of parents' wishes and practices.

Developing a culture within the setting that values difference and diversity is an important part of modelling the values that we seek to nurture within the children. Establishing an ethos where all are welcome and valued is a key element in developing a sense of community and in establishing a community within and around the setting. When considering these elements it is appropriate for us to think about the six different areas covered in a single equalities policy (namely: age, ethnicity, disability, gender, religion/belief and sexuality) and to consider the appropriateness and application of each in developing a welcoming and inclusive setting.

A further example (Woolley, 2008: 115) illustrates the point from another perspective:

> A former colleague recounted to me the story of a child in Year 1 who drew his family during a lesson focusing on 'Our Homes.' He drew his mum, who he lived with, and his two dads; mum and dad had separated not long after he was born, and dad now lived with his male partner. His teacher asked who the second man was, and when told responded: 'We don't want to see that here.' She told the child to rub out his father's partner.

Here, the teacher devalues the child's family community with the implicit message that the child's experience lacks validity or value. As professionals we must remember that children to not choose the circumstances of their birth or the composition of their families; it is our role to value their experience of family and to show that we respect where they come from. This is important not only for the child but in order to model respect and inclusion to all children.

Practical tasks

Plan an open afternoon (or similar) to enable parents and carers to visit your setting, based around a current theme being explored by the children.

As you prepare, consider:

- strategies to involve and engage carers and parents;
- how you can encourage the visitors to meet each other and to get to know new people;
- how you can use this as an opportunity to learn more about parents' skills and interests, with a view to involving them as helpers in the setting.

After the event, evaluate:

- its success in reaching parents and carers;
- what barriers may have affected participation and how you will develop opportunities with those unable to attend;
- how you can utilize the knowledge and skills of carers and parents in the setting;
- the range of strategies you have in place to communicate with carers and parents and whether these are effective.

Using experiential learning

Experiential learning is implicit to much of what we do in the Early Years Foundation Stage. It works on two levels. First, providing children with experiences through which they learn, for example, going on visits, meeting visitors, engaging in role-play and activity-based learning. Second, it involves using the children's prior experience, knowledge and understanding as a basis for next steps, for example, through sharing accounts of a birthday celebration, a visit to the seaside, helping to plant seeds on the allotment or helping with the housework. Essentially this involves using experience from two directions: experience that we provide for the children; and experience that they bring to the setting.

I observed one example of experiential learning in a Reception class in a school in Nottinghamshire. Iona's mother, Mrs Jackson, was visiting the class as a part of Book Week: a series of activities planned to promote the enjoyment of books and to encourage children to share books with their parents. Mrs Jackson was sitting with a small group of children to share one of her favourite fairytales. She read extracts from the story and asked the children to describe the pictures and say how they thought the characters felt. Mrs Jackson's copy of the book included text in Braille, which she read to the children. Through the activity they were able to appreciate how she could read the text and understood that she had a special way of reading using her fingers to follow the text. She explained to the children, 'There are lots of different ways of reading. You can read the story using the writing, some people follow the story using the pictures and I can read the story in Braille.' The children were able to share the book and try 'feeling' the text of the story. They were fascinated by Mrs Jackson's ability to interpret the embossed page. Making links with people with different abilities gives children an appreciation of diversity and how a variety of needs are approached. Including people with varying abilities, skills and talents in our setting helps to foster an inclusive ethos and to develop children's respect for others. Developing links with parents and carers is essential and is explored in Chapter 2 as a part of developing children's self-esteem and providing a welcoming and supportive environment in our setting.

Learning in community also brings the opportunity to solve problems with the support of adults or more capable peers. Vygotsky (1978) termed this the *zone of proximal development*. The zone is the distance between the actual development of the child and the level they are able to achieve with support. Rather than revealing the fruit of a child's development, their achievement judged in retrospect, the zone shows the prospective achievement of the child: the buds of development. Learning alongside others provides an opportunity to develop a sense of community through shared experience and the development of relationships.

Addressing stereotyping

Stereotypes are a kind of shorthand that judges individuals according to labels that may derive from their gender, ethnicity or some other characteristic. They make a generalization about a person without taking into account the individual character, abilities or other attributes of that person. As was noted in Chapter 2, common gender stereotypes are that boys show instrumental traits (e.g. competitiveness and assertiveness) and girls show more expressive traits (e.g. care, sensitivity and being considerate) (Williams and Best, 1990). Other stereotypes may include the notion that parents and carers from some backgrounds are more supportive of their children, that some children have shorter attention spans or cause more disruption, that children with poor behaviour have lower ability or that certain traits infer a person's sexual orientation. As professionals it is our role to develop a setting in which children's interests and personalities are not limited by stereotyping.

As professionals it is our role to make informed judgements based in evidence: we assess children, note their achievements and identify next steps for their development. It is essential that such formative assessment is not affected by preconceptions based on gender, ethnicity, social class or any other factor. When the Foundation Stage became a part of the National Curriculum in 2002, the existing baseline assessment was replaced with a profile, based on the early learning goals, which involved practitioners' ongoing assessment of the six areas of learning. Many of us will be familiar with this process, where summary profiles have to be completed for each child reaching the end of the Foundation Stage (at age 5 years) in England. An evaluation of this new process undertaken by Ofsted (2004) found that it was less sophisticated than the previous method and did not provide the same information. It was based on the day-today observations that a professional makes of individual children when they are involved in activities in the usual classroom environment; there were no tests or set tasks for the Foundation Stage Profile. Assessment was thus based on professional judgement, which can be subjective Gillborn (2008: 116; 117). argues that black pupils were judged to be less successful using this process than in the previous system. This would suggest that teacher stereotypes were affecting the assessment of learners. This idea was supported by Dianne Abbot MP, speaking in a debate on black and minority ethnic pupils in the House of Commons (Abbott, 2008):

In relation to base-line entry tests, black pupils outperform their white peers at the start of school, but the new observation-based foundation stage profile reverses that pattern. Black pupils are disproportionately put in bottom sets, and as someone whose child went through the school system and went to a state primary close to my home in Hackney, I have seen that with my own eyes. The following is an interesting quote from a Department for Education and Skills report, 'Evaluation of Aiming High: African Caribbean Achievement Project': 'Whilst many teachers . . . believed setting to be based solely on ability, data indicated that African Caribbean pupils were sometimes relegated to lower sets due to their behaviour, rather than their ability.'

It is possible that assessment can establish inequality and that it can maintain it. It is essential to value all learners and to ensure that our teaching and assessment methods take into account their learning styles and needs so that a sense of community where all are valued and equal is established and maintained (Woolley, 2010). We need to identify and challenge stereotypes and to reflect on our own values and attitudes to ensure that we model the fairness and acceptance that we seek to engender in our learners (Connolly, 2003). This is fundamental to enabling all children to learn and to achieve (DfES, 2004). Sometimes this can lead to soul searching and while this process is not easy or pain free ultimately it will lead to more inclusive practice.

Conclusion

This chapter has explored some of the ways in which communities are diverse. We all know that each child in our care is a unique and special individual. In order to value this we need to value their home backgrounds and to show an appreciation for where they come from. While some families will live lives very different to our own, it is not our place to judge their choices: rather we need to offer support and to seek to understand their circumstances and wishes for their child. This is particularly key when considering issues of belief. We cannot presume to know what parents or carers believe and need to work in partnership so that we can be sympathetic to their views when caring for their children. We also need to address stereotyping and ensure that children are appreciated as unique individuals.

The local community can provide a rich source of knowledge and skills to support learning. Working alongside others will help children to appreciate difference and diversity and to understand that we depend upon one another in many ways in day-to-day life. All people exist in community: it is impossible to exist in total isolation in the contemporary world. Even a person who produces all their own food, collects their own water, generates their own electricity and refuses to own a telephone, radio or television is affected by the air quality resulting from the behaviour of others. No one can be totally unaffected by others. Thus a sense of community is important as we seek to live in ways that show respect and care for those around us. Appreciating the importance of responsibility and respect for others is an essential part of the learning we share with our children.

References

Abbott, D. (2008) Speech on Black and Minority Ethnic Pupils, House of Commons. Hansard Column 224WH 1 April 2008. Available at: http://www.publications.parliament.uk/pa/cm200708/cmhansrd/cm080401/halltext/80401h0009.htm#08040154000587

Berger, K. (2000) *The Developing Person: Through Childhood* (2nd edition). New York: Worth Publishers

Berk, L. (2006) *Child Development* (7th edition). Boston, MA: Pearson Education

Connolly, P. (2003) 'The development of young children's ethnic identities', in C. Vincent (ed.) *Social Justice, Education and Identity*. London: RoutledgeFalmer

DCSF (2008a) *Statutory Framework for the Early Years Foundation Stage*. London: Department for Children, Schools and Families

DfES (2004) *Every Child Matters: Change for Children in Schools*. London: Department for Education and Skills

Gillborn, D. (2008) *Racism and Education: Coincidence or Conspiracy?* London: Routledge

Griffiths, J. and Pilgrim, Tony (2007) *Picnic in the Park*. London: British Association of Adoption and Fostering

Lindon, J. (1993) *Child Development from Birth to Eight: A Practical Focus*. London: National Children's Bureau

Morris, J. and Woolley, R. (2008) *Family Diversities Reading Resource*. Lincoln: Bishop Grosseteste University College Lincoln

Ofsted (2004) *Transition from the Reception Year to Year 1: An Evaluation by HMI*. London: Ofsted. Available from: http://www.ofsted.gov.uk/Ofsted-home/Publications-and-research/Browse-all-by/Education/Key-stages-and-transition/Key-Stage-1/Transition-from-the-Reception-Year-to-Year-1-an-evaluation-by-HMI

Piaget, J. and Inhelder, B. (1969) *The Psychology of the Child*. New York: Basic Books

Selman, R. L. (1980) *The Growth of Interpersonal Understanding*. New York: Academic Press

Thomas, R. (2005) *Comparing Theories of Child Development* (6th edition). Belmont, CA: Wadsworth

Vygotsky, L. S. (1962) *The Thought and Language*. Cambridge, MA: MIT Press

Vygotsky, L. S. (1978) in M. Cole, V. John-Steiner, S. Scribner and E. Souberman (eds) *Mind in Society*. Cambridge, MA: Harvard University Press

Williams, J. E. and Best, D. L. (1990) *Measuring Sex Stereotypes: A Multi-nation Study*. Newbury Park, CA: Sage

Woolley, R. (2008) 'Development, well-being and attainment', in M. Cole (ed.) *Professional Attributes and Practice: Meeting the Standards for QTS*. London: Routledge

Woolley, R. (2010) *Tackling Controversial Issues in the Primary School: facing life's challenges with your learners*. London: Routledge

Conclusion

The series editors and authors hope that you find this book of interest and use to you in your professional work. If you would like to read more about the subject area, we recommend the following reading and websites to you.

Further reading

Dowling, M. (2005) *Young Children's Personal, Social and Emotional Development* (2nd edition). London: Paul Chapman Publishing

Hohmann, M. and Weikart, D. P. (2002) *Educating Young Children* (2nd edition). Ypsilanti, MI: High/ Scope Press

Johnson, J., Nahmad-Williams, L., House, A., Cooper, L. and Smith, C. (2009) *Early Childhood Studies.* Harlow: Pearson Education

Riley, J. (ed.) (2003) *Learning in the Early Years; a Guide for Teachers of Children 3–7.* London: Paul Chapman Publishing

White, M. (2008) *Magic Circles: Self-esteem for Everyone through Circle Time.* London: Sage

Useful websites

British Association for Early Childhood Education: resources, advice and publications www.early-education.org.uk

Citized: information about developing citizenship education across different phases of the education system www.citized.info

The Family Diversities Reading Resource: 100+ picture books for children, published by Bishop Grosseteste University College Lincoln www.bishopg.ac.uk/fdrr

Multiverse: a website addressing the educational achievement of pupils from diverse backgrounds www.multiverse.ac.uk

PSHE Association: information and resources to help to develop children's personal, social, health and economic education www.pshe-association.org.uk

National Healthy Schools Programme: www.healthyschools.gov.uk/

National Healthy Schools Programme: www.healthyschools.gov.uk/

Outdoor Learning from Learning and Teaching Scotland: http://www.ltscotland.org.uk/earlyyears/
about/currentissues/outdoorlearning/introduction.asp

www.behaviour4learning.ac.uk

www.emotionaldevelopment.co.uk

www.high-scope.org.uk

www.parentinguk.org

www.pre-school.org.uk

www.surestart.gov.uk

www.teachernet.org.uk

www.understandingchildhood.net

If you would like to read more about other key areas of the Early Years Foundation Stage, please see the following:

Communication, Language and Literacy, by Callander, N. and Nahmad-Williams, N. (London: Continuum, 2010)

Creative Development, by Compton, A., Johnston, J., Nahmad-Williams, L. and Taylor, K. (London: Continuum, 2010)

Knowledge and Understanding of the World, by Cooper, L., Johnston, J., Rotchell, E. and Woolley, R. (London: Continuum, 2010)

Physical Development, by Cooper, L. and Doherty, J. (London: Continuum, 2010)

Problem Solving, Reasoning and Numeracy, by Beckley, P., Compton, A., Johnston, J. and Marland, H. (London: Continuum, 2010)

Index